THE WORLD STEAM TRAIN
ALBUM

THE WORLD STEAM TRAIN
ALBUM

JOHN WESTWOOD

MAGNA
BOOKS

Published by Magna Books
Magna Road
Wigston
Leicester LE18 4ZH

Produced by Bison Books Ltd
Kimbolton House
117A Fulham Road
London SW3 6RL

ISBN 1-85422-571-5

Printed in Hong Kong

PAGE 1: No.28 of the Sierra RR in California, a preserved 2-8-0 that has featured in several Hollywood productions.

PAGE 2 (ABOVE): A typical US six-wheeled switcher, now preserved at Traveltown in California.

PAGE 2 (BELOW): A 'Royal Hudson' of the Canadian Pacific, still used for excursions in British Columbia.

PAGE 3: "Sir Nigel Gresley," one of the London and North Eastern Railway's record-breaking A4 Pacifics.

BELOW: A Shay locomotive, popular in America for forestry lines.

RIGHT: "Flying Scotsman," perhaps the world's best-known locomotive, hauling an excursion.

BELOW RIGHT: "Green Arrow," a mixed-traffic version of "Flying Scotsman," hauls an excursion in the north of England.

STEAM'S GOLDEN AGE

In 1914 almost all of the world's rail systems made the bulk of their income from freight operations. Railroads were, and would remain, ideal carriers of bulk commodities, the raw materials of industrialization. There were companies like the Taff Vale in Wales and the Virginian in the United States that were virtually coal conveyor belts, and most other companies operated slow, heavy trains carrying coal, ores and grain.

There were also fast freight trains, but before 1914 these were largely confined to North America and Britain. The US and British governments had not prevented the building of several competing lines linking specific points so that, for example, between London and Manchester, or New York and Chicago, there were several companies offering very similar routes. The intense competition expressed itself not in price reductions but in quality of service,

LEFT: The early days of the transcontinentals; an office of the Atlantic & Pacific, which later became part of the Santa Fe RR.

BELOW: "Wm. Crooks," a 40-ton 4-4-0 which in 1862 pulled the first passenger train out of Minneapolis.

ABOVE RIGHT: Many US 4-4-0s have been preserved. This one is commemorating the 'last spike' ceremony of America's first transcontinental in 1869.

BELOW RIGHT: The Lake Shore RR, later part of the New York Central, advertises its service to the Mid-West.

and fast-freight systems were often the result of this competition. But not always, for some traffics could only move if the railroad provided a fast service and, as every company was seeking to expand its traffic, special trains for fish, milk, and other perishables were run regularly. By the outbreak of World War I it was also possible to see fast freights operating in those countries where the governments had created railroad networks that were not based on competition.

The picture was similar with passenger services. Many passenger trains were slow because high speeds often produced little extra revenue and simply raised operating costs. On the other hand, the passenger train was a company's shop window, and public reputation was important for business.

In the competitive environments of the US and Britain, passengers tended to patronize the trains providing the fastest service, but this was not always the case. Not only could brand loyalty be important, but comfort, courtesy, and punctuality also played a role. Between Chicago and New York, the New York Central and the Pennsylvania Railroads fought over the elite clientele with their 'Twentieth Century Limited' and 'Broadway Limited,' but lesser companies also took a share of the traffic by emphasizing or inventing a particular desirable quality. The

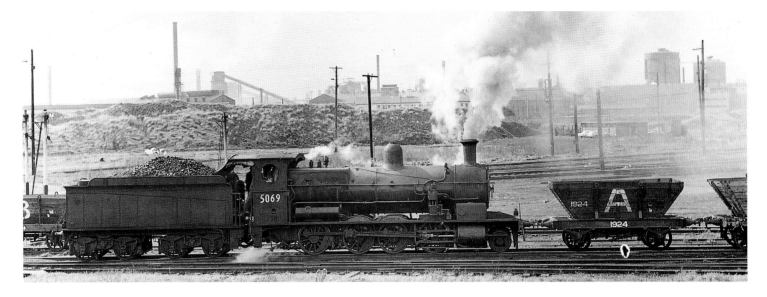

Lackawanna Railroad, for example, for years successfully persuaded passengers that it was less smoky than the other lines, publicizing its mythical heroine Phoebe Snow and the hard coal that its locomotives burned. In Britain, two consortia of companies, the East Coast and West Coast, fought for the Anglo-Scottish traffic and even indulged in perilous races during which each strove to reach the destination first. Then a third company, the Midland Railway, entered the market with a longer route and attracted a good clientele by providing well-advertised extra comfort.

Suburban passenger traffic had grown rapidly in

the late nineteenth century, but it was never very profitable because of low-fare period tickets, and excess capacities in off-peak hours. Short-distance freight trains, at a time when most stations had their own freight yard, had high costs but were indispensible for local communities. Moreover, such services acted as feeders for the long-distance freights and for that reason were not unprofitable. The assembly, re-assembly and break-up of freight trains that took place in main sorting yards was an activity with high costs and absolutely no revenue, but was an essential part of freight-train operation. Part of the expense of switching freight cars at the end of their runs was often borne by the clients themselves, who ran their own industrial railroads. Many mines, docks and steelworks had very big railroad systems, usually served by small locomotives with short wheelbases that could negotiate the sharp curves that characterized such lines.

Railroad construction had slowed down but not ceased by the end of the nineteenth century. Localities that did not have a railroad were still demanding one, and many of the lines built in the early twentieth century were simply map-fillers. Some of them were main lines, like Britain's Great Central Railway from Sheffield to London and the last American transcontinental, the Milwaukee Railroad. Both these paralleled other, older, companies and neither was really necessary. To survive, they were strong on innovation but nevertheless were among the first to disappear when both America and Western Europe were pruning their railroad mileages.

ABOVE LEFT: Coal traffic in New South Wales; wooden-bodied low-capacity cars can be seen, although the picture dates from as late as 1971. The locomotive is of a Beyer Peacock turn-of-the-century design, some units of which were built in Australia and others imported from England.

LEFT: One of the many Phoebe Snow posters published by the anthracite-burning Lackawanna RR to persuade clients that its locomotives were clean-working. This railroad was one of several competing for New York-Chicago traffic.

BELOW LEFT: The 'Forney Tank' was a locomotive designed for short-distance commuter runs. It carried water in a rear tank and could run equally well in both directions. It was popular in the US, but in Britain and elsewhere the side-tank locomotive was preferred.

ABOVE RIGHT: Wheat exports from Victoria, Australia. At this period no special vehicles were provided and most freight handling was manual. The railway was an essential element in opening up new grain areas.

RIGHT: The 4-6-0 wheel arrangement came to Britain later than in the US and initially took the form of the Highland Railway's 'Jones Goods.' This example was built in 1894 and lasted until 1939.

LEFT: The Atlantic, or 4-4-2 wheel arrangement, never gained the popularity of its successor the 4-6-2. But in England the Great Northern built two series for fast passenger trains. This is "Henry Oakley," of the original, smaller, type.

BELOW LEFT: The railway age was also the age of manufacturing, and manufacturers knew that railway stations were one of the best places to advertise. Enamelled signs like this remained in place for years, sometimes decades, with the advertiser paying an annual rent.

ABOVE RIGHT: In Britain, passenger vehicles were resplendent and well-kept. This example is from the North Eastern Railway, a mainly coal-hauling company.

RIGHT: Even after motor trucks had appeared the railways continued to handle perishables by passenger train. Milk, carried in churns like these, was loaded and unloaded at countless British stations every day.

For localities that offered little traffic but which had the political or financial power to demand railroads, start-up costs could be considerably reduced by adopting a narrower gauge. This prevented the through-running of vehicles over the mainline network but, if it was a question of narrow-gauge railroad or no railroad at all, the narrow gauge was acceptable. Such lines were seen in the American Rockies, in Ireland, in French and German country districts, in Australia but, above all, in India, where in the late nineteenth century a complete network of meter-gauge lines had been built to fill in the gaps between the existing broad-gauge routes.

By 1914 the locomotive was still clearly a descendant of the 'Rocket,' but it was a link in principal only. Locomotives had not simply grown bigger, but had changed in almost every detail. Some changes resulted from new materials, but most developments came from an urge for improvement.

The move from wrought iron to steel that had started in mid-century, while benefiting the track most of all, had also produced locomotives that lasted much longer, were easier on maintenance, and were lighter per unit of power. They also performed better, because steel wheel on steel rail was a harder contact; this is why some locomotives which had had their tires replaced performed better in old age than when new.

By World War I, the superheater had been accepted as essential for hard-working locomotives and especially for mainline passenger engines. It consisted of an arrangement of tubes in the smokebox that enabled steam on its way between the boiler and cylinders to be reheated. This brought it to a very high temperature that avoided condensation as it cooled inside the cylinder. The superheater thereby enabled much more power to be derived from a given expenditure of fuel and water.

The superheater was probably the most important innovation in locomotive technology since the age of Stephenson. Many attempts had been made to develop such a device, because the need had been clearly seen for decades, but it was the German Wilhelm Schmidt ('Hot-steam Willy' to his friends) who developed a design that could survive the rough ride of a locomotive.

Another approach to efficient steam utilization was the compound locomotive, in which the steam was used twice, first in one or two high-pressure cylinders and then in one or two bigger low-pressure cylinders. This avoided the steep drop in steam temperature of simple (non-compound) locomotives. The respective merits of superheating and compounding were argued about until the end of steam. The French, in particular, favored the compound, whereas the Americans and, usually, the British, preferred simple-expansion engines. In Britain, the exceptions were the Midland Railway, which built very successful three-cylinder compound passenger engines, and the London & North Western Railway, which built some highly unsuccessful compound locomotives for both passenger and freight service.

Compound loocmotives were more expensive to build and maintain, but in terms of pure efficiency, as the French were beginning to show by 1914, a locomotive that had both compounding and super-

heating was the best. In Germany and Russia the 'cross-compound' was popular. This had a large outside low-pressure cylinder on one side which took steam exhausted from the small high-pressure cylinder on the other. It was said to be economical, but designers never quite solved the problem of equalizing the thrust of the left-hand and right-hand cylinders at all speeds.

Industrialized countries had their own locomotive works and the split between US and British design traditions dated from before 1850. The frames of American locomotives were built up from steel bars, whereas British locomotives had frames machined from steel plate. American locomotives were visibly different from British types because, as some Britons put it, 'they were built inside-out.' Nowadays the term 'accessibility' would be used to describe the American preference for exposing as much as possible of the locomotive's functional parts. In Britain, all possible pipework and, almost always, the cylinders were concealed. This produced a much smoother outline, an effect of modesty and decency, that American locomotives lacked. But the American locomotives with their outside cylinders and valve gear did not require their mechanics to perform as contortionists.

Although the US possessed the most locomotives, they were not standardized. It was in Germany and Russia that specific locomotive designs were built in the largest numbers. By 1914 the Royal Prussian State Railway covered the greater part of Germany, and could therefore order locomotive classes in very large numbers. About 3500 of its passenger 4-6-0 locomotive, later known as the Type 38, were eventually built. This was an enormous number compared with Britain, with its many railroad companies each building locomotives of their own exclusive design, and where only a few classes exceeded 100 units. But Russia, where most companies were state-owned and even the private companies

RIGHT: A mixed-traffic 0-6-0 of the London and South Western Railway ends its days performing yard work for British Railways.

BELOW LEFT: 'Camel-back' and 'Mother Hubbard' cabs appeared on US locomotives fitted with special wide or sloping fireboxes to burn particular kinds of coal. Such fireboxes did not present a suitable surface for the controls, so the engineer drove from a special cab, while the fireman remained in the usual position. This Union Pacific 4-4-0 was built in 1887.

BELOW: This 0-6-0 tank locomotive, of the small and simple 'Terrier' class, was built for the London Brighton and South Coast Railway for passenger work. Several have been preserved in Britain and North America.

LEFT: The 2-8-0 tank locomotive was an unusual type, but the Great Western Railway built it for heavy short-distance freights like this one in the South Wales coalfield.

RIGHT: The Prussian P8 4-6-0 was built by the thousand and a few have survived into the 1990s, although not in Germany. This one is hauling a secondary service in Romania.

BELOW: The compound locomotive was never especially popular in the US or Britain, partly because its first cost was greater and it needed careful driving and maintenance. Probably the most successful was the 'Midland Compound' 4-4-0, of which this locomotive is a late example. It is shown hauling a local train out of Birmingham in the 1950s.

were under pressure to buy standard designs, did even better than Germany. The standard Russian 0-8-0 cross-compound, the Type O, was built by a number of works and would finally total about 8000 units.

Most industrialized countries had their own locomotive works, and by 1914 German, American and British builders dominated the export markets, although other countries like France, Switzerland and Belgium also had their share. Britain was unique in that all the bigger railroad companies had their own works, producing engines for the one company. The other British builders had a few orders from home railroads but were very dependent on export markets. While they had no tight monopoly in the British Empire (Canada did not buy British; some Australian states were beginning to build their own locomotives; and New Zealand was ready to buy American as well as British engines), British manufacturers were favored by most British overseas railroads, including the large Indian companies. Argentinian railroads, largely British-owned, were also a good market.

With few exceptions, and notably the Pennsylvannia and Norfolk & Western Railroads, US companies bought their motive power from the big locomotive-building companies. This market was dominated by three big outfits: Baldwin, American Locomotive (Alco) and Lima. Lima was the smallest and youngest of these and, not surprisingly, would be the most innovative in the postwar years. In Canada, the Canadian Pacific built some of its own, American-style locomotives, and it bought some from one or other of the Canadian locomotive works, as did the other Canadian companies.

Although different railroads, and different countries, had different requirements for their locomotives, there was a certain amount of technology transfer. In Britain, the Great Western Railway in the years preceding 1914 acquired French compound locomotives for study and in the process adopted some French design details, while deciding that the extra trouble of compounding was not worth the gain in efficiency. The Great Western Railway (GWR) also studied US practice, and it could be argued that the range of very superior locomotives that the GWR was building by 1914 owed its success to a willingness to blend the best French, US and British engineering. Sometimes the mixture was taken to extremes; the GWR's 'Bulldog' class of 4-4-0 lasted until the 1950s with its American-style taper boiler perched on archaic outside frames.

New wheel arrangements tended to be seen first in America, simply because at each stage of development it was the US railroads that required the bigger designs. In 1914 Britain, the 2-8-0 was the biggest freight engine, and very few railroads possessed this type. Some had the 0-8-0, which were ideal for heavy haulage but, like the 0-6-0, did not react very well with the track. Most British companies were content with the 0-6-0, and the Midland Railway was so reluctant to build bigger locomotives that it often assigned two of these small engines to its coal trains, a highly uneconomic practice. In Scotland, the Highland Railway had shown one way forward by building 4-6-0 locomotives for freight work.

In the US, freight locomotives with 10 driving wheels, 2-10-0s and 2-10-2s, were well-established by 1914 and were already too small for some railroads. For this reason American builders had been designing Mallet-type engines. With the driving wheels and cylinders divided into two pivoted groups, as many as 16 driving wheels could be used without coming to grief on sharp curves.

RIGHT: A 'Bulldog' 4-4-0 of the Great Western Railway. This was of unusual design, combining heavy outside frames with a slender American-style taper boiler, but the class lasted for fifty years. It is shown hauling a secondary service to Stratford-upon-Avon in 1949.

BELOW RIGHT: British railways for over a century built the inside-cylinder 0-6-0 for mixed-traffic work. It was a simple and trouble-free machine, although not the best for smooth riding. This is one of the most successful designs, the 'Dean Goods' of the Great Western. Introduced in the 1880s, the class survived until the 1950s, and some were sent abroad in both world wars.

LEFT: Right up to 1922 the Midland Railway used 4-4-0 locomotives for its London-Scotland trains, despite the heavy loads. This immaculate, crimson-painted, machine is hauling a similarly resplendent train of nine clerestory-roofed cars. The smokebox numberplate was a Midland feature that was copied first by the Midland's successor, the London Midland and Scottish Railway, and then by British Railways.

LEFT: The 'single' locomotive train with its one driving axle was long a favorite for British fast trains. Its tall driving wheels meant that the mechanism moved slowly, which was essential with the primitive lubricants then used. Here a Great Northern 4-2-2 hurries north out of London with the 'Flying Scotsman' in 1890.

BELOW LEFT: The 4-4-0 was justifiably known as the 'American' type and was long used in North America for passenger and freight. The three examples seen here are testing Devil's Gate Bridge during the construction of the Union Pacific RR.

BELOW: Australian officials and dignitaries show the courage of their convictions as the new Moorabool Viaduct is tested in 1894. The Victorian Railways locomotives are both 0-6-0 units of typical British design, although it was becoming the practice to build locally some units of each order.

RIGHT: Mixed gauge in Portugal. Portuguese main railroads were built to the 5ft 6in gauge of the neighboring Spanish railroads, but such lines were too expensive for local routes, so meter gauge was also used. Here a meter-gauge Mallet locomotive crosses a mixed-gauge viaduct.

LEFT: Mixed gauge on the Great Western Railway. Until Parliament put an end to it, this British company used the expensive but advantageous 7ft gauge. This picture shows the third rail added to form a standard gauge track.

BELOW: Mixed gauge at Merida in Mexico. Here the lines are standard gauge and the American narrow gauge of 3ft. Both the locomotives shown here are US-built; the nearest is a narrow gauge 2-6-0 supplied in the 1920s while the standard gauge 4-6-0 was built by Baldwin in the 1880s.

LEFT: Mixed gauge in the Sudan. The British favored 3ft 6in gauge for their African railways, with the idea of one day having a 'Cape to Cairo Railway.' But the Sudan also had a short-lived standard-gauge line and an extensive 2ft-gauge system serving the cotton growers.

ABOVE: Mixed gauge in South Africa. The first railways in the Cape were of standard gauge, but then it was decided that only a narrow gauge could penetrate inland through the mountains. 3ft 6in was chosen, and for some years the old standard gauge lines were fitted with a third rail.

RIGHT: This 1891 Great Western Railway locomotive was designed to be easily convertible from broad to standard gauge.

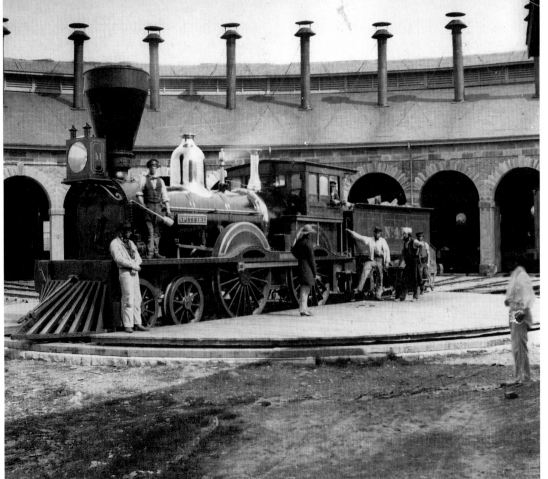

ABOVE: The 2-4-0 was favored by the British railways for passenger service before being ousted by the 4-4-0. This is one of the simple designs built by the London and North Western Railway for its mainline services. "Hardwicke," the locomotive shown, broke records in the inter-company 'Race to Scotland' and has since been preserved.

LEFT: In the early years the Canadian railways did buy some engines from England. This is "Spitfire," supplied to the Great Western of Canada in the 1850s. It is of 5ft 6in gauge, because the Canadian government mistakenly imposed that gauge in the beginning. By the time standard gauge was adopted in 1873 the GWR of Canada was buying American-style locomotives.

RIGHT: This locomotive was less fortunate than "Hardwicke," illustrated on the left. It was of the same class, but spoiled its good looks by derailing at excessive speed and hitting an overbridge. This was the Ditton Junction accident of 1912, which took 15 lives and was caused by the use of a locomotive crew that was unfamiliar with the line.

BELOW: One of the longest-lived 2-4-0 types was that of the Great Eastern Railway. This unit lasted until the 1950s, and is shown hauling a local train out of Cambridge.

ABOVE LEFT: The 'Pennsylvania Limited' at the turn of the century, when the competition for high-class traffic between New York and Chicago was becoming intense. This luxury train was the Pennsylvania RR's challenge to the New York Central.

LEFT: A 4-4-0 of the Central Pacific equipped for fire-fighting; the availability of water and high pressure steam made the locomotive very suitable for this purpose, but few were equipped because the need was small.

ABOVE: A classic American 4-4-0 of the 1880s, posing on the turntable at the Southern Pacific's Monterey roundhouse. Until the advent of the 4-6-0, and then the 4-6-2, the 4-4-0 hauled most American passenger trains.

RIGHT: As late as the 1970s it was possible to see 4-4-0s and 2-4-0s working alongside each other in Indonesia. The 2-4-0 here is just short of its century, having been built in Scotland during the 1880s. The larger 4-4-0, about thirty years younger, is of German construction. For some reason this former Dutch colony rarely bought Dutch-built locomotives, preferring German, Swiss, and sometimes American, in the twentieth century.

FAR RIGHT: This Southern Pacific 4-4-0 was photographed to mark the departure of the SP's first train fitted with the Westinghouse automatic brake. The introduction of this brake in the 1890s made operation safer and enabled fast freight trains to be introduced.

BELOW RIGHT: One of the last regular American 4-4-0 duties was this branch service in New Brunswick. Here the locomotive takes water halfway along its daily trip between Norton and Chipman in 1957.

LEFT: "Caleb Balderstone," one of a sturdy Scottish 4-4-0 class bearing names from Walter Scott's novels, built for the North British Railway in 1914 and still active on secondary services in 1953.

RIGHT: Another Scottish 4-4-0. This big-boilered machine was built for the Caledonian Railway in the early 1920s and is shown leaving Greenock Pier in the 1950s. There were basic similarities between this 4-4-0 and the NBR 4-4-0 opposite. They were of about 60 tons and both had 78-inch driving wheels.

BELOW: This British 4-4-0, built in the 1880s for the London and South Western Railway by Beyer Peacock of Manchester, differs from the two Scottish designs, being smaller and having outside cylinders.

ABOVE: Another classic British 4-4-0 of 1920s vintage; a 'Director' of the Great Central Railway preparing to take a British Railways train out of Cleethorpes in 1951. When young these locomotives worked fast trains out of London and, thanks to their free-steaming boilers, were held to be the equal of a 4-6-0.

LEFT: An outside-framed 'Duke' 4-4-0 built by the Great Western Railway in the 1890s. Intended for the hilly lines of Devon, it ended its days in Central Wales, where it was photographed on a local freight train in 1949.

RIGHT: One of the later American 4-4-0s. This example hauled passenger trains for the Pennsylvania RR, and is now preserved.

LEFT: The LMS Railway, which absorbed the Midland Railway in 1922, was still building MR locomotive types at the end of that decade. In this 1948 photograph of a Derby train preparing to leave the old New St. Station in Birmingham, the 4-4-0 is still less than twenty years old. In Britain the position of the light indicated the class of train: the single oil lamp placed high on the smokebox indicates a stopping train.

RIGHT: The best-known Midland Railway 4-4-0s were the three-cylinder compounds. Here one of them leaves Bradford, Yorkshire, making a trial run for the new 1925 service.

BELOW: This is how the Midland Compounds looked when they were first introduced in the early years of the century. No. 2633, built in 1905, is shown passing through hilly Derbyshire, ideal terrain for compounds, which performed best with steady hard work.

ABOVE: A North Eastern Railway 0-6-0 of the 1880s. Six-wheelers like this were maids-of-all-work on the British railways. Most had driving wheels of about 5ft diameter, enabling them to tackle secondary passenger trains as well as freight.

LEFT: In North America the 0-6-0 wheel arrangement was used primarily for purpose-built yard locomotives, like this Pennsylvania RR example. The slope of the tender was to improve the view of the enginemen when coupling.

48

ABOVE: An outside-frame 0-6-0 of the Midland Railway, dating from the 1870s. This particular locomotive lasted 61 years, with some rebuilding.

RIGHT: One of the numerous Z.19 0-6-0 locomotives of the New South Wales Government Railways, introduced in 1877. Although of British design, this particular locomotive was built in Australia and was in service until the 1970s.

ABOVE: A heavy 0-8-0 switcher of a type designed by the United States Railroad Administration during World War I. Slightly ahead of its time when built, this design was adopted by many companies after the war.

LEFT: One of the numerous 0-8-0 cross-compound locomotives built for most of the Russian railroads in the late nineteenth century. Several thousand were built before they were succeeded by an even more numerous 0-10-0.

BELOW: An 0-8-0 of the London and North Western Railway. A few British railways adopted this wheel arrangement for heavy freight work, but most remained with the 0-6-0 or preferred the more steady 2-8-0. These eight-wheelers were used only for mainline freight services, unlike the American, which were confined to switching, or the Russian, which often appeared on passenger trains.

LEFT: In Britain the Great Western Railway was the first big user of the 2-8-0 type. The 2800 class locomotive shown here belonged to a series of innovatory designs introduced in the first decade of the century and incorporating some American features like the taper boiler and prominent smokebox saddle.

BELOW LEFT: In the US the 2-8-0 appeared earlier than in Britain and, unlike the British 2-8-0, had a short reign as the prime freight locomotive. It became useful for branch and local work and was a favorite for short lines. This Boston and Albany example was built in 1893.

BELOW: This Australian 2-8-0, seen under a timber-built coaling stage at Newcastle in New South Wales, was one of a class designed in Britain in 1896 and used largely for coal traffic. Almost three hundred were built. Their second and third pairs of driving wheels were flangeless, to aid negotiation of sharp curves.

ABOVE: A 4-8-0 of the Queensland Railways. The 3ft 6in gauge system favored this wheel arrangement, probably because the leading truck gave a better ride on light track.

LEFT: The South African railways also liked the 4-8-0 wheel arrangement, for similar reasons.

RIGHT: The 4-8-0 was rare in the US. This locomotive was of a class built for the Illinois Central RR in the 1890s. The IC had considerable colliery traffic and the 4-8-0, although inferior to the 2-10-0 in haulage capacity, rode better over sharp curves.

BELOW: "El Gobernador," built by the Central Pacific in its own workshops at Sacramento, was at the time (1883) the world's biggest locomotive. A 4-10-0 for pusher service, it suffered from insufficient boiler capacity and a tendency to derail on switches, despite the sideplay of the rear driving wheels (which was accommodated by ball joint bearings in the coupling rods).

LEFT: The Canadian Pacific, with its difficult Rocky Mountain section and long freight drags elsewhere, was an early user of the 2-10-0. This example was photographed at Calgary toward the end of its life in 1957.

BELOW: For many years the only British locomotive with ten coupled wheels was this four-cylinder 0-10-0, built for pusher service on the Lickey Incline in Worcestershire. However, toward the end of the steam era British Railways acquired some very successful 2-10-0 locomotives.

ABOVE: The 1914 'Triplex' of the Erie RR had three engine sets, unlike the standard Mallet design, which had two. Thus there were three cylinders visible on each side. Most Mallet locomotives had a forward, pivoted, engine unit and a rear, fixed, unit. The wheel arrangement of this monster was 2-8-8-8-2, and those 24 coupled wheels constituted a world record.

RIGHT: The Mallet concept was originally designed for small tank locomotives using sharply curved track, and in Europe many were built in this form. Some of them, like this one, still work regular services on narrow-gauge lines in the former GDR.

ABOVE: The Mogul, or 2-6-0, was another example of American practice favored by Britain's Great Western Railway. The GWR built hundreds of this design, which largely superseded its 0-6-0 for mixed-traffic work. The picture shows one of these units pulling a freight through Birmingham in the 1950s.

ABOVE: The Canadian National Railways inherited a mixed collection of 4-6-2 types from its constituent companies. Here, one of them takes a Malbaie train out of Quebec's Palais Station in 1958.

LEFT: One of the outstanding 4-6-2, or Pacific, types was the Pennsylvania RR's K4. Introduced on the eve of World War I, it continued in mainline service until the 1950s. This example was photographed as late as 1957, when it was used for secondary services to Atlantic City.

LEFT: The Kitson-Meyer type had two engine units beneath a single boiler, like a Mallet, but had a girder frame and different positioning of the cylinders. It was built in Britain in very small numbers for export; this example was photographed in the Argentine.

BELOW LEFT: Industrial railways were to be found mainly in mining and forestry areas. This is a scene on a British quarrying line near Kettering, Northamptonshire in 1962, showing iron ore loaded on tip wagons.

BELOW: The Shay locomotive was another design that provided a flexible wheelbase. It was a favorite among logging companies, although the example shown was used by the Bolivian State Railroad. The power trucks were free to rotate, and vertical cylinders turned a crankshaft coupled to rotating shafts that transmitted their motion to the wheels through bevel gears.

BELOW: Of all the narrow-gauge articulated locomotives the Fairlie was the best-known. It was designed for twisting, narrow-gauge railways, enabling high power to be exerted without a long rigid wheelbase. It had two pivoted power bogies, and two boilers back-to-back with a single firebox. This example was built for New Zealand in 1872.

ABOVE: A rival of the Shay locomotive was the Heisler, pictured here. It differed from the Shay in that its gears connected with the axles rather than the wheel rims. Charles Heisler had the first unit built in 1894, having failed to persuade the Baldwin Company to back him.

LEFT: Industrial locomotives had short wheelbases so as to negotiate sharp curves, and this was especially necessary for dock locomotives. This example was built by the Great Western Railway, but followed the design of locomotives originally built for a Cornwall mineral railway. It is shown at work in Plymouth docks.

ABOVE: Welsh slate quarries used distinctive locomotives with cut-down profiles that enabled them to move close to the rock and into low tunnels. Hard-working and unsophisticated, they were very much a basic locomotive, not even offering a cab to their one-man crew. Large quarries elsewhere used standard gauge railways, but the Welsh preferred the narrow gauge.

65

THE RISE AND FALL OF STEAM

After World War I, railroad managers in the victorious countries were intent on 'getting back to normal,' but things could never be the same again. Government control of US and British railroads had in many cases brought more efficient operation, demonstrating that the division of a rail network between a large number of private companies had disadvantages. Nationalization to create unified state rail systems was advocated by many, but the political climate was not right for that. In the US, competition rather than coordination was again the rule and the railroads were thereby weakened in their response to highway competition and to trade union strength. One legacy of wartime government control, not experienced in Britain, was the appearance of standard (USRA) locomotives, specified and ordered by the US Railroad Administration and bought by several companies. But this initiative in locomotive standardization was not continued after the end of the war.

In Britain, 123 companies were compelled by the government to amalgamate into four big corporations, the London Midland and Scottish (LMS), the London and North Eastern (LNER), the Southern (SR), and the Great Western (GWR) – the only company to retain its identity. This amalgamation took place in 1923, the same year as the Canadian railroads were restructured. In place of one large profitable company (Canadian Pacific) and several smaller and unprofitable companies, there was created a unique two-company system, with the private CPR competing with a state corporation, Canadian National Railways, that had been created by merging the unprofitable lines. In locomotive matters, the CNR was soon setting the pace, introducing US-size 4-8-4 and 2-10-2 locomotives to Canada.

In France, the mainline railroads were nationalized in 1938, creating French National Railways (SNCF). In Russia and Germany, the railroads were reformed into state corporations, the Russian state

LEFT: On the eve of the diesel age; the Santa Fe RR's 'Chief' toils up Raton Pass behind three locomotives.

TOP RIGHT: "Saint Bartholomew," a Great Western 'Saint' 4-6-0, arrives in London Paddington with the Cheltenham Spa Express on its 1923 record-breaking run of 77 miles in 71 minutes.

ABOVE RIGHT: One of South Africa's crack trains, the 'Union Express,' hauled by a large-boilered 4-8-2 locomotive. Despite the 3ft 6in gauge, South African speeds and train weights were little different from those of standard gauge.

RIGHT: At the close of the steam age, Canadian National parades several generations of motive power.

railroads subsequently becoming the world's biggest. In Germany, the new Deutsche Reichsbahn served the whole country but was really an enlarged version of the former Prussian State Railway. Only in countries far removed from the war did the picture seem to be unchanged. British companies, their headquarters in London, continued to operate most railroad mileage in India and Argentina. South Africa already had its unified system, but in Australia the gauge question still dominated a country in which each state controlled and operated its own railroad system.

During the war, national armies had trained thousands of truck drivers, and after the war they sold off their surplus vehicles at bargain prices. Small, often one-man and one-truck, highway transport companies began to compete for the railroads' merchandise and other high-rate traffic. By the 1920s, the railroads of America and Europe were already fighting back with new fast-freight trains, a process that affected locomotive design. In Britain, the mixed-traffic locomotive of the 2-6-0 and 4-6-0 types became popular, not only because they were capable of hauling most passenger trains but also because they were ideal for fast freight. The GWR built its 'Hall' 4-6-0 class and in the 1930s the LMS introduced the 'Class 5,' an improvement on the 'Hall.' Meanwhile, the LNER preferred the large-boilered 2-6-0 before producing the large V2 2-6-2 whose performances became legendary. In the US, the Lima Locomotive Company, answering the need for

engines that could maintain high horsepower at fast speeds, introduced its 'Superpower' range of locomotives, starting with a 2-8-4, and then a 2-10-4. These locomotives had a large firebox, which was made possible by the supporting four-wheel truck.

Other American large-firebox types were the 4-6-4 and 4-8-4. The 4-8-2 and 2-8-2, long favored by American railroads, remained popular but the 4-6-2, or 'Pacific,' type began to fall from favor for the fastest trains. Among several exceptions to this general trend was the Pennsylvania Railroad's K4 4-6-2, which hauled mainline passenger trains up to dieselization. The K4 had been designed before 1914 but was later equipped with a mechanical stoker; a human fireman lacked the the stamina to feed the high horsepower of which some engines were capable. Mechanical stokers soon became standard equipment for the bigger American locomotives, while in the USSR during the same period this problem was being solved by establishing the three-man locomotive crew.

When buses and coaches captured short-distance suburban passengers, or the sparse country traffic, it was not a great blow to the railroads, for whom such passengers quite often represented a financial loss. But in the 1920s the private car and the long-distance bus began to make sizeable inroads into rail passenger services.

The railroads responded to this competition by providing more comfort. This implied heavier trains and bigger locomotives, which is why the 4-6-4 superseded the 4-6-2, and the 4-8-4 the 4-8-2 in the US. Then, in the 1930s, they began to offer high speeds, largely to create a more modern image. Streamlining, although it was said to be worthwhile

TOP: Another of the London Brighton and South Coast 'Terrier' 0-6-0 tank locomotives, awaiting light duties in about 1920.

ABOVE: Trains to the very top of Scotland started from this station at Inverness. An LMS Railway Class 5 4-6-0 pulls out with the morning train in 1951 to take this long route which, unusually for Britain, was singletrack. In the background can be seen the locomotive workshops of the former Highland Railway, which originally owned the line.

RIGHT: A long freight crosses the Starucca Viaduct of the Erie RR in Pennsylvania. The two leading locomotives are assisted by a pusher in the rear, whose exhaust can be seen in the distance.

ABOVE: For its singletrack main line across the Mendip Hills, the Somerset and Dorset Joint Railway acquired a small class of 2-8-0 locomotives. Here is one of them approaching Bath with a fast freight.

ABOVE RIGHT: This class of Canadian Pacific light 4-6-2 was built in the 1940s but followed closely an earlier design. The train is at St Jerome, on one of the long branches north of Montreal.

RIGHT: The Victorian Railways in Australia provide a veteran 0-6-0 for a recruiting train during World War I.

at over 80 mph (128 km/h), was very much a public relations gesture.

All the same, some remarkably fine locomotives were created beneath the streamlining. It was a British streamlined Pacific, 'Mallard' of the LNER, which won the all-time authenticated speed record for steam locomotives at 126 mph (200 km/h). From the mid-1930s, the LNER and LMS were operating streamlined trains between London and Scotland, and the LNER 'Silver Jubilee' between London and Newcastle was not only fast, but offered very smart lightweight passenger cars with strikingly modern interiors.

In the US, the Milwaukee Railroad built some streamlined engines for its Chicago-St. Paul service in 1935. These were a reversion to the old 4-4-2, or 'Atlantic,' wheel arrangement, which was very suited to fast running, being easier on the curves. When the trains became popular and therefore heavier, the 4-4-2s were replaced by 4-6-4s, but not before the concept of high-speed locomotives with just four driving wheels had caught on elsewhere. The Canadian Pacific and Baltimore & Ohio Railroads acquired 4-4-4s, an unusual arrangement that provided a large firebox for maximum horsepower, together with a wheelbase suitable for high speed. It seemed to work well, but the concept of the short and fast train was undermined by the scarcity of routes

over which such trains could profitably operate. A similar fate overtook the Class 12 streamlined 4-4-2s introduced by the Belgian Railways for the Brussels-Ostend run. These were highly unorthodox, having inside cylinders to which access could be gained through wide apertures in the streamlined casing. They were in service only for a few months before World War II put an end to high-speed trains in Belgium.

As it turned out, the Canadian speed record was won not by a CPR 4-4-4, but by a Canadian National 4-6-4, and it was the 4-6-4, in the shape of the 'Royal Hudsons,' that became the CPR's prime passenger locomotive. Other American railroads, notably the New York Central (NYC), favored the 4-6-4, but in Britain the type was limited to a single unit on the LNER, and in France to a handful of experimental locomotives. However, in Australia the Victorian Railways made a success of the type, acquiring 70 of the 'R' class in the 1950s. In Britain and Germany, the Pacific type was favored for the faster trains, although the GWR stuck to the 4-6-0 arrangement. In France, Pacifics were supplemented by 4-8-0 and 4-8-2 locomotives on the more difficult routes. South African Railways also favored the 4-8-2, while Russia entrusted most of its passenger trains to small 2-6-2 engines, but in the 1930s introduced its 'Iosif Stalin' type, which closely resembled the US 'Superpower' 2-8-4.

After World War II the USSR built its type P36 4-8-4, and that wheel arrangement was also chosen by Spanish National Railways for its '242F' class,

ABOVE LEFT: Surprisingly, streamlining gripped many railroads. Even the Manchurian railroads followed the fashion, although the locomotive shown here had very little opportunity of reaching the speeds that streamlining could help.

ABOVE: The Chesapeake and Ohio RR shifted massive loads of coal to Lake Erie and used huge locomotives to do it. A train of empties approaches on the left, while a 2-10-4 hauls a loaded train on the right. The picture was taken at Limeville, Kentucky, in 1947.

ABOVE RIGHT: The 4-6-4, or Hudson type, was favored by several American railroads, including the Canadian Pacific. This CP locomotive, shown leaving Montreal in 1960, was of an early design that was well-liked and which was later developed into the 'Royal Hudson' class.

RIGHT: The 4-8-4 was a rarity in Europe, but the Spanish National Railways acquired a few for their heaviest passenger trains. This is one of them in 1969, awaiting its next duty at Zaragoza. The class was claimed to be Europe's biggest passenger locomotive type.

claimed to be Europe's heaviest passenger locomotive. In the US, the NYC built what was possibly the highest development of this wheel arrangement, the 'Niagaras' of 1946. The longest-surviving American 4-8-4 design was the 'QR-1' series supplied to Mexico in 1946, which was still at work well after steam traction had been abandoned in the US.

In France, locomotive performance was revolutionized by the research of Andre Chapelon, who showed that the typical French compound locomotive could produce vastly more horsepower if treated to a number of fairly inexpensive modifications: bigger superheaters, free-flow steam passages, and scientifically derived draughting exemplified by the Kylchap double chimney that was fitted to a growing number of French passenger locomotives.

In those countries where bigger railroad corporations had been established there could be a high degree of locomotive standardization. In Britain and Germany, successful classes were built in hundreds of units. The LMS Class 5, for example, eventually totaled more than 800. In Germany, the most widespread type was eventually the 'Kriegslok' built during World War II. This was a 2-10-0 derived from a prewar freight 2-10-0 design and was used not only in Germany but in German-occupied Europe. It totaled about 6000 units, but was outnumbered by the standard Soviet 0-10-0, of which about 11,000 examples were built.

For Western Europe, the 2-10-0 was a large engine, although France built several series for coal traffic. In Britain, the three biggest companies relied on the 2-8-0 for their heaviest freight trains. The LMS, in addition, had some of the 'Garratt' patent articulated locomotives. This layout, consisting of a boiler and cab pivoted between two wheel and engine

ABOVE: Another of the GWR's 2-8-0 tank locomotives for heavy short-distance freights. It is shown entering Cardiff in South Wales, where numerous mineral branches converged on the main line. During the Depression of the 1930s the GWR, to create work, rebuilt some of these as 2-8-2 tank locomotives, with a bigger coal capacity.

LEFT: One of the Chapelon Pacifics of French National Railways (SNCF). This is one of the locomotives rebuilt from an older and less effective class of 4-6-2; the 'Kylchap' double chimney is clearly visible. It is hauling a train out of Paris to the north.

ABOVE: The 'Royal Scot' of the West Coast Route was one of Britain's best-known trains and linked London with Glasgow. It is shown here climbing Beattock Bank, one of two severe climbs faced by northbound trains. The locomotive is one of the LMS 'Coronation' class Pacifics, "City of Lichfield." Engines of this class produced the highest horsepowers obtained from British locomotives, but nevertheless a pusher locomotive has been provided on this day.

RIGHT: "Rhyl," a 4-6-0 rebuilt by Stanier of the LMS Railway, takes the best London-Liverpool train, the 'Merseyside Express,' through the London suburbs.

RIGHT: A Union Pacific RR 'Challenger' 4-6-6-4, now preserved. This design was a further development of the Mallet concept, being suited for passenger as well as freight haulage, although it was mainly used for the quite fast and quite heavy freights operated to and from the Rockies.

BELOW: The 3-cylinder 'Jubilee' 4-6-0 type was built for passenger service by the LMS Railway and three have been preserved. This is "Leander," shown hauling an excursion.

BOTTOM: Another view of "Leander." The maroon livery was chosen by the LMS for its main passenger locomotives, and was derived from the style used by the Midland Railway, one of the constituent companies of the LMS.

units, was essentially two engines in one, providing high power, a light and well-spread axleload, and an easy ride on curves. Railroads in the British Commonwealth, with the notable exception of Canada, were the biggest users of the Garratt type and the designs produced for East Africa and New South Wales, together with one unit for the USSR, were the biggest engines built in Britain.

US railroads, however, did not buy Garratts, preferring further enlargement of the Mallet type, which was also an articulated (jointed) machine providing the power of two engines in one. The biggest examples were on the Union Pacific Railroad (UP), where the 'Challenger' type was used for hauling freights over the rising grades into the Rockies. In the 1940s, the UP bought even bigger Mallets, the 'Big Boy' 4-8-8-4 type, which were destined to be the biggest steam locomotives ever built.

The Union Pacific also possessed some 4-12-2 units. Apart from an unsuccessful 4-14-4 built in the USSR, these represented the ultimate development of the rigid-frame freight engine. Twelve coupled wheels were definitely too many for all but the more easily curved lines. An articulated design was really needed for more than 10 driving wheels.

The 2-8-2 was a useful general-purpose locomotive, performing in America the secondary tasks that in Britain might be entrusted to a 2-6-0 or 0-6-0. The latter wheel arrangement, so common in Britain, India and Australia, was used in North America only as a yard locomotive. This was another difference between American and British practice.

RIGHT: Inside a British locomotive depot. This is Blyth, on the former North Eastern Railway, and the locomotive is one of the large 0-6-0 design introduced by that company for its coal traffic in 1906. The picture was taken in 1965, three years before the end of British steam traction.

BELOW RIGHT: The Great Northern Railway of Ireland was a late purchaser of compound 4-4-0 locomotives. The five units of class V were introduced in 1932 and one of them has been preserved in working order.

Whereas British railroads, and to a lesser extent other European systems, favored 0-6-0 tank locomotives for yard work, in America 0-6-0 tender locomotives were built for this job. Other countries were content to entrust their yard work to old freight locomotives retired from mainline service.

In Europe, especially Britain, and in India and Australia, the tank locomotive was much more common than in America, being widely used for commuter trains. As cities gave birth to outer suburbs and dormitory towns, bigger tank locomotives were needed to haul commuter trains that could travel out 30 miles (48 km) or so from the cities. The LMS built some fine 2-6-4 tank engines for this work, while even bigger engines were used in France, culminating in the massive 2-8-2 of the 141TC type used by the SNCF for services out of the Gare du Nord. In North America, steam commuter trains were usually entrusted to older mainline locomotives, as was the case with the final two such operations, the CPR's in Montreal and the Grand Trunk Western's in Detroit.

World War II put an end to some outstanding locomotive projects. Both the LMS and LNER in Britain were planning bigger versions of their passenger locomotives, while Chapelon in France had some remarkable locomotives on the drawing board, only two of which were completed – a 2-12-0 freight engine and a massive 4-8-4, 242A.1, with triple chimney and high horsepower. Neither of these received proper trials and development before electrification overtook the French railroads.

In the US, the diesel locomotive had become well-

established in the war years and was being sought by most railroads. Eventually, in the late 1950s, the last big railroad with steam traction, the Norfolk and Western, decided to dieselize, and this was followed by the end of steam traction on the Canadian railroads.

In Britain, the railways were finally nationalized in 1948 and the new British Railways immediately decided to build a new range of standard locomotives. The most interesting of these was the 2-10-0, a wheel arrangement unusual for Britain. One of this very successful class, "Evening Star", was the last steam locomotive built by British Railways, which ended steam traction in 1968.

It was not until the 1970s that steam was finally ousted in Australia, France, West Germany, and most other European countries. Of these, the New South Wales Government Railway had most convincingly proved the longevity of the steam locomotive, for in the 1970s it was still operating its type Z.19 0-6-0 locomotives, built in Britain in the 1870s.

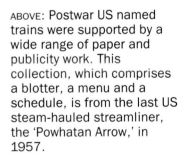

ABOVE: Postwar US named trains were supported by a wide range of paper and publicity work. This collection, which comprises a blotter, a menu and a schedule, is from the last US steam-hauled streamliner, the 'Powhatan Arrow,' in 1957.

LEFT: After the end of British steam traction, "Lord Nelson," a 4-cylinder 4-6-0 of the Southern Railway, was one of the locomotives preserved and used for steam excursions. It is shown here in the north of England, far from its original London-Bournemouth route.

RIGHT: An 0-6-0 tank locomotive, originally built by the LMS for yard work, finds post-retirement employment on one of Britain's steam tourist lines, the Keighley and Worth Valley Railway in Yorkshire.

BELOW: In 1968, the last year of British steam traction, a Class 5 4-6-0 of the former LMS is used on a parcels train. Hundreds of these useful mixed-traffic locomotives were built by the LMS and its successor British Railways, and more than a dozen have been preserved.

PREVIOUS PAGE: "Flying Scotsman" in excursion service. This 3-cylinder 4-6-2 locomotive has hauled excursions in the US and Australia as well as Britain.

ABOVE: The 'Panama Limited' of the Illinois Central RR ran almost the whole north-south length of the US, from Chicago to New Orleans. It is shown here behind a 4-6-2 locomotive supplied by Brooks in 1916.

BELOW: The 4-6-2 became known as the Pacific because it was first ordered by the Southern Pacific RR in 1904. The SP had a number of heavy trains passing over easily graded routes and believed this wheel arrangement was the most suitable. The locomotive shown was built by Baldwin after World War I and was a development of the original design.

ABOVE RIGHT: The Pacific type soon became popular in the US, and later in Europe and elsewhere. This is a variant supplied to the New York Central, a company which also ordered Pacifics with smaller driving wheels for freight work.

RIGHT: Large Pacifics like this design for the Boston and Albany RR represented the limit; further power increases required the 4-6-4 wheel arrangement.

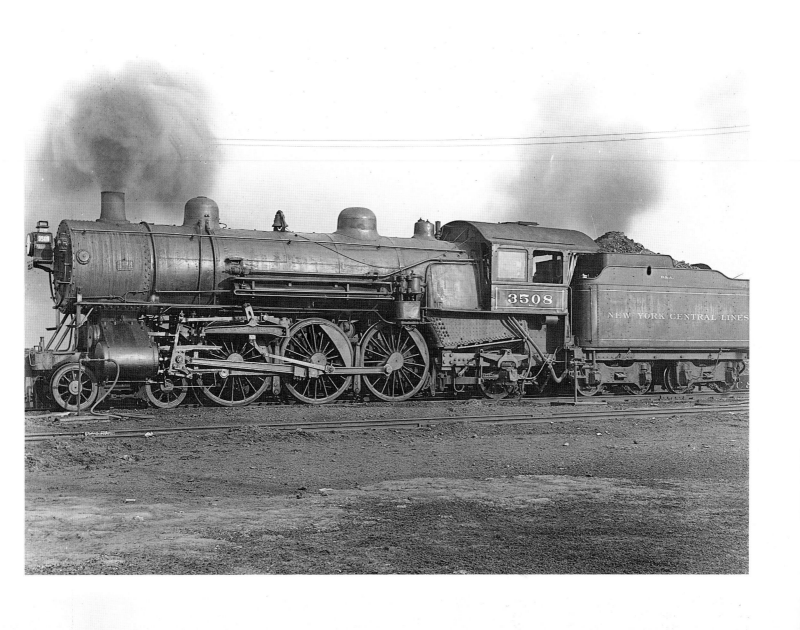

One of the large Pacifics built by Canadian Pacific and reflecting the styling of the streamline age. The class was built to haul most of the fast passenger trains but when the picture was taken in 1957 it was confined to commuter service at Montreal.

LEFT: Another view of a Canadian Pacific large 4-6-2. Painted maroon and pale gray, these locomotives retained their fine appearance even when relegated to commuter service. The CPR also built a 2-8-2 version for fast freight work, but that was painted black.

BELOW: This French compound Pacific, waiting to work the 'Golden Arrow' Paris-London service, is very different from the American idea of a 4-6-2. It was more economical in terms of coal consumption per horsepower-hour, but required careful maintenance and operation.

TOP RIGHT: "City of Lichfield" on the turntable at Carlisle. This was one of the LMS 'Coronation' class, sometimes known as the 'Duchess' class. These powerful 4-cylinder Pacifics hauled the heavier passenger trains on the West Coast London-Scotland line. Some were originally streamlined to haul the pre-war 'Coronation Scot' train. The yellow stripe on the cabside was to remind crews that they might be operating under overhead electric catenary.

CENTER RIGHT: One of the London and North Eastern Railway's Pullman trains leaving the London suburbs in 1938. The locomotive "Enterprise" is of the same design as "Flying Scotsman." The class still hauled the more important trains even after the coming of its streamlined development, the A4 class. They were powerful and fast locomotives but, like some other British Pacifics, were liable to slip when starting on wet rails.

BOTTOM RIGHT: The 'Royal Scot' changes engines at Carlisle, one 'Duchess' giving way to another. The left-hand locomotive was the last of the class to be built (in 1947) and had roller bearings.

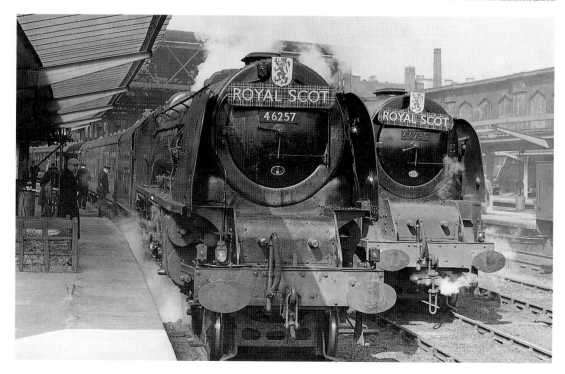

RIGHT: A pair of New South Wales Government Railways C-38 Pacifics. These were designed and built in Australia and the first five were streamlined. They were introduced in 1943 and there were 30 in the class. No.3813, in the right of this 1970 picture, has been preserved.

BELOW: A Queensland Railways 4-6-2. This 3ft 6in gauge class was mainly built in the railway's own workshops and handled the faster passenger services as well as seasonal fruit trains. One hundred were built, and several have been preserved.

BELOW RIGHT: "Robin Hood" was one of the 2-cylinder 'Britannia' Pacifics introduced by British Railways in 1951, soon after nationalization. The new BR classes were intended to include the best features from the locomotive practice of the four companies that were nationalized but in fact LMS practice prevailed. It was a capable class totaling 55 units, designed for a future of poor coal and poor maintenance.

LEFT: Westbound trains at Southampton in 1951. While older London and South Western locomotives handle the local trains, an 'air-smoothed' Southern Railway Pacific is watered for the final stage of its run to Bournemouth.

BELOW LEFT: Another of the postwar 'Britannias,' "Dornoch Firth," takes the 'Thames-Clyde Express' out of Carlisle. This long-established train had its roots in the old Midland Railway's struggle to win passengers for its London-Scotland route.

BELOW: After World II the LNER designed new Pacifics for the East Coast main line. This is one of them, "Abbotsford," hauling the Pullman 'Queen of Scots.' These locomotives were the direct and final descendants of "Flying Scotsman" and its class.

LEFT: One of the rebuilt 3-cylinder Pacifics that the Federal German Railways used for the last steam-hauled long-distance trains. This is a Kiel-Cologne train leaving Hamburg in 1967. The German railroads, unlike the British and most of the American, introduced electric and diesel traction slowly, prolonging the useful life of the more modern steam locomotives.

BELOW: An elderly Pacific inherited by the Canadian National Railways helps with secondary passenger services from Stratford, Ontario, in 1959. Cold weather that January required the restoration to service of many steam locomotives, partly for snow clearance and partly to supplement hard-pressed diesels.

ABOVE: In the German Democratic Republic steam traction lasted longer than the state itself, although mainline passenger services like this Dresden-Berlin train were dieselized by 1980. The 4-6-2 locomotive belongs to one of the several standard classes designed between the wars by Richard Wagner, and is distinguished by the wide gap between the rear driving wheels and the trailing truck; evidence that the designer knew the importance of unrestricted airflow to the firegrate.

LEFT: One of the Canadian Pacific's postwar light 4-6-2s curves through the Quebec countryside in 1962.

RIGHT: CPR light Pacific No.1256 is prepared for the road at Trois Rivieres, on the Montreal-Quebec main line.

BELOW LEFT: Another veteran from the Canadian National Railway's collection of Pacific designs sets out from Quebec City with a train to Richmond in 1958.

BELOW RIGHT: Another CPR light Pacific takes an Ottawa-Toronto train beneath the federal parliament buildings in 1957.

BELOW: One of the original CPR light Pacifics brings the Fredericton branch train into the New Brunswick capital in 1958.

ABOVE: A smartly turned out WP Pacific awaits its next duty at New Delhi in 1963. At that period most of the Indian broad gauge long-distance trains were handled by these postwar locomotives.

BELOW: Tumpat locomotive depot, at the northern end of the meter-gauge Malaysian Railways eastern main line. All the locomotives are from a class of 40 3-cylinder Pacifics imported from Britain after World War II and having 54in driving wheels.

RIGHT: Another WP Pacific, allocated to India's Southern Railway (hence the brown paintwork, in contrast to the green of the Central Railway's WP illustrated above). This unit is of a batch manufactured in Canada and the US in 1949.

TOP RIGHT: Although some streamlined Atlantic, or 4-4-2, locomotives were built for the Milwaukee RR in 1935 for high-speed services, the wheel arrangement was not generally favored (except for a short period before the advent of the Pacific). This Atlantic was built for the Illinois Central RR in 1903.

CENTER RIGHT: The Baltimore and Ohio RR and the Canadian Pacific combined the free-running capability of the Atlantic with the large firebox of the 4-6-4 to arrive at the unusual 4-4-4 wheel arrangement. This is one of the Canadian examples.

BOTTOM RIGHT: Perhaps the most successful and long-lasting Atlantics were those of Britain's Great Northern Railway. These were built before 1914 and, after superheating, achieved some fine performances. Some lasted until the 1950s.

LEFT: One of a small class of unique high-speed 4-4-2 locomotives built for the Belgian State Railways on the eve of World War II. They had inside cylinders, access to which was through apertures cut in the sides. Originally intended for the Brussels-Ostend service, they had little chance to show their paces. One has been preserved.

97

LEFT: A very distinct type of 4-4-0, the Great Western 'Bulldog.' This is "Seagull," withdrawn in 1954 and the last to remain in service. Inside cylinders were normal for British 4-4-0s, but outside frames were unusual.

BELOW: One of the London and South Western Railway's 'Greyhound' 4-4-0s hauling a named train for British Railways in Devon. The class was introduced in 1899 and the picture dates from 1961. The train is a detached part of the 'Atlantic Coast Express.'

ABOVE: Possibly the most accomplished 4-4-0 ever designed was the 'Schools' class of the Southern Railway. This 3-cylinder design was introduced in 1930 and performed as well as the 4-6-0s. This is "Shrewsbury" tackling a train from London to the south-west in 1962, shortly before the withdrawal of the class.

BELOW: One of the longest surviving North American 4-4-0s is prepared for the road at Chipman in New Brunswick in 1957. The Canadian Pacific kept three 4-4-0s here, for service on the branch to Norton.

LEFT: A Southern Pacific RR Ten-wheeler of 1882 typifies the rugged construction and design of the American 4-6-0 type. This locomotive, built by the Schenectady Locomotive Works (predecessor of Alco), lasted 40 years.

CENTER LEFT: Toward the end of the steam age, surviving 4-6-0 locomotives were associated with rural branchlines. This is a Canadian National example in 1957, on light duties at Charlemagne, Quebec.

BOTTOM LEFT: Another CNR 4-6-0, this time on a regular passenger service, the daily Victoriaville-Montreal train, in 1958. It is at Bridge Street, the last station before Montreal.

ABOVE RIGHT: In Britain the 4-6-0 hauled main passenger trains right up to the end of steam. This is "Hackworth," of a small class rebuilt by the Southern Railway from large 4-6-2 tank locomotives made redundant by electrification.

RIGHT: On the eve of nationalization in 1948 "Royal Scots Grey" halts at Shap with a London-bound train. This 3-cylinder 4-6-0 was rebuilt in 1945, acquiring its taper boiler; in this form, it became one of the 'Rebuilt Scot' class.

LEFT: In Britain, signal lamps burned oil, so periodic deliveries of oil were made to signal cabins. Here a Class 5 of the former LMS Railway is engaged in this duty. It is 1967, and steam traction has only one more year. Previously this duty would not have been performed by a 4-6-0, but by a smaller locomotive.

BELOW: This powerful-looking Pennsylvania RR 4-6-0 is interesting because it was built specifically for commuter service at a time when few US railroads were still buying this wheel arrangement. Commuter services, with their frequent stops and their need for fast acceleration, really required a specially designed locomotive, but most American railroads preferred to use elderly locomotives retired from first-line service.

LEFT: A morning scene at London's Liverpool Street Station in 1925. The nearest locomotive is a 4-6-0 of the former Great Eastern Railway, which had just been amalgamated into the new London and North Eastern. The locomotive heading the train of close-coupled four-wheelers is a 2-4-2 tank.

BELOW: "Royal Sovereign," the 4-6-0 allocated to the royal trains, fills in time with an ordinary Cambridge-London train in 1956. The first locomotive of the class was named "Sandringham" after the royal residence.

RIGHT: A pair of 4-6-0s leave Cambridge with an Ipswich train in 1956. They are of the GER type illustrated in the top picture opposite, but they have been rebuilt with larger boilers. The doubleheading was a convenient way of returning a spare locomotive back to its home depot.

TOP: A 4-6-0 of the New South Wales Government Railways in 1970. This class was obtained by rebuilding 4-6-4 tank locomotives made redundant by electrification in Sydney.

CENTER: A Canadian Pacific 4-6-0 in rural surroundings.

ABOVE: A highly sophisticated 4-6-0: a Nord Railway compound as operated by French National Railways in the 1950s. Introduced in 1907, this type had two outside high-pressure cylinders, with two larger low-pressure cylinders beneath the smokebox.

RIGHT: A 'Castle' 4-cylinder 4-6-0 at Wootton Bassett, a station on one of Britain's oldest main lines (London-Bristol). The 'Castles' were the outstanding passenger locomotives of the GWR and set records hauling, among others, the 'Cheltenham Flyer.'

ABOVE: The Great Western Railway in the late 1940s. As railwaymen exchange greetings, "County of Merioneth," a 2-cylinder 4-6-0, tops Dainton Summit in Devon with a train bound for the Midlands. The 'County' class was the last of the GWR 4-6-0 designs, being introduced in 1945, and only 30 were built.

LEFT: The lightest of the GWR 4-6-0 designs was the 'Manor' class. Here "Frilsham Manor" leaves Carmarthen in South Wales. With their light axle-load, the 'Manors' could bring modern traction to lightly-laid secondary lines. Thirty were built.

TOP RIGHT: The 'Grange' class was the GWR's intermediate mixed-traffic 4-6-0, being bigger than a 'Manor' but smaller than a 'Hall.' Here "Blakemore Grange" hauls a train from Devon to the Midlands in 1949.

CENTER RIGHT: "Sir Daniel Gooch," a GWR 'Castle' 4-6-0, photographed at the same location as the preceding picture and with a similar train. For most passenger services, mixed-traffic locomotives like the 'Halls' and 'Granges' were just as useful as the bigger 'Castles.'

BELOW: A 'Hall' climbs toward Birmingham with a train from London. This design was the first of the classic British 4-6-0 mixed-traffic locomotives introduced in 1928, although this locomotive, "Cory Hall," was built in the late 1930s. 'Halls' had 72in driving wheels, 'Castles' 80in, and 'Granges' and 'Manors' 68in.

LEFT: A 2-cylinder 'King Arthur' class 4-6-0 of the Southern Railway. These were named to commemorate characters and features of the King Arthur tales, because they originally hauled trains to Cornwall, King Arthur's homeland. This unit, "Sir Hervis de Revel," built in 1925, had since been fitted with a multiple-jet exhaust.

BELOW: One of the numerous P8 4-6-0 locomotives originally built for the Prussian Royal State Railway but also used in Poland and Romania and, as war reparations, in Belgium and France.

ABOVE: Perhaps the best-looking of the British 2-cylinder mixed-traffic 4-6-0 designs was the LNER B1 class, introduced during World War II and of which over 400 were built. This is "Mayflower," which is now preserved.

RIGHT: "King Richard I" of the GWR. The 30-strong 'King' class was an enlarged edition of the more numerous 'Castle' reserved for the heavier trains. Both classes were very successful for their time, but their performance was improved after they had been fitted with double chimneys toward the end of their lives.

LEFT: This 4-6-0 is hauling the last regular steam passenger train in New South Wales in 1970. It is of a type designed by Beyer Peacock of Manchester and supplied from 1892, with a total of 191 entering service. Twenty of them were built by Baldwin in the US and another twenty by the railway's own Sydney workshop.

BELOW: "Barfleur," one of the 3-cylinder 'Jubilee' 4-6-0 class of the LMS, designed to haul all but the heaviest fast passenger trains of that company. Built from 1934, this class also totaled 191 when construction ceased.

RIGHT: One of the always-useful Class 5 4-6-0s of the LMS helps a 'Rebuilt Scot' with a heavy West Coast train in the 1950s. This busy main line from London to the North-west was the first British trunk route to be electrified. During this period flatbottom rail was laid on the fast tracks, but the slow tracks still had the traditional British 'bullhead' rail.

BELOW: "Earl of Birkenhead," another of the GWR 'Castle' locomotives, brings a London-Wolverhampton train into Birmingham. Several units of this class have been preserved, some in working order.

LEFT: The British railway scene in 1954. Departure time at Liverpool's Lime Street Station. The stock is painted in the maroon and cream styling favored at that time by British Railways for its long-distance trains. The engine is blowing off steam; this shows that there is full pressure in the boiler, but in the more disciplined prewar days such wasteful displays were frowned upon.

RIGHT: A badly parked car brings traffic to a halt on the Southern Railway's Dover Docks line in 1937. The irate railway flagman (trains had to be preceded by a red flag) is waiting alongside the car.

RIGHT: Gleneagles Station in 1927. The train is hauled by a 'Midland Compound.' Railway amalgamation, with the new LMS and LNER companies absorbing the Scottish lines, meant that English designs could appear in Scotland. The first amalgamation plan had proposed a self-contained Scottish Railway, but this was rejected.

RIGHT: Day-trippers disembarking at the seaside resort of Weston-super-Mare. The GWR built a special station, adjoining the existing one, to handle holiday traffic here. The date is about 1925 and the train is hauled by a new 'Castle' locomotive.

BOTTOM RIGHT: Race traffic was carefully planned in Britain. Here the Southern Railway is coping with the Derby at Tattenham Racecourse station. The date is 1922, and evidently some middle-aged Pullman cars have been provided.

ABOVE LEFT: The Italian State Railways was one of the few systems favoring 2-6-2 tender locomotives. Here, one of them pulls away from Verona with a Venice-Milan train.

ABOVE: The 2-6-2 was a very convenient wheel arrangement for tank locomotives, the truck at each end smoothing the ride in both directions, and the rear truck supporting the coal bunker. This example was owned by the Great Western Railway.

LEFT: A very different design of 2-6-2 tank locomotive is this American narrow-gauge unit. Some of these were supplied by Baldwin in 1898 for the 2ft 6in gauge railways of Victoria, Australia, and others were built locally to the same design. This is part of the narrow-gauge system at Wangaratta.

ABOVE: The biggest user of the 2-6-2 tender locomotive was Soviet Railroads. This Su class was built for more than thirty years and was a modification of a tsarist design. Train speeds were not high in Russia, and the Su was suited to steady running over flat routes, hauling heavy passenger trains.

RIGHT: The Santa Fe RR also owned some 2-6-2 locomotives. This example is now preserved at the State Railroad Museum in Sacramento, and was photographed while hauling a replica of the 'Coyote Special,' Death Valley Scottie's record-breaking Los Angeles-Chicago train. The occasion was a television program celebrating the fiftieth anniversary of the run.

ABOVE: The 2-6-2 was also used in Hungary, and after the dissolution of the Austro-Hungarian Empire this example was allotted to the new Yugoslavia. A cross-compound, it was photographed in the 1970s, hauling a local train in Croatia.

BELOW: In the US the 2-6-2 was known as the 'Prairie' type, because that was where it first appeared. This is the first, built by Baldwin in 1901 for the Hannibal and St. Joseph RR in Missouri.

RIGHT: Possibly the most outstanding 2-6-2 design was the V2 of Britain's LNER. Designed for mixed traffic and especially fast freight, the class was capable of handling the heaviest passenger trains. The "Green Arrow" seen here was so named to mark the introduction of the railway's 'Green Arrow' express package-freight scheme.

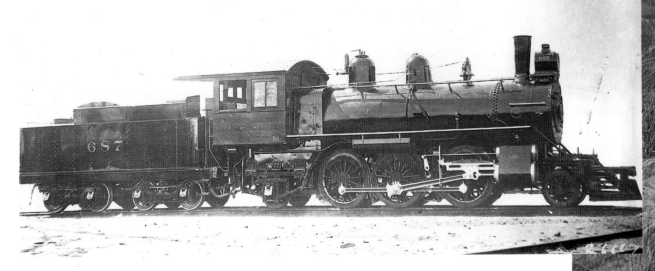

ABOVE: The most handsome development of the 2-10-4 was the 'Selkirk' class of the Canadian Pacific, designed for the heavy grades of the Rockies. With their 63in driving wheels they could deal with passenger as well as freight trains. This is one of them hauling the 'Dominion' in the Bow River Valley, Alberta.

LEFT: The Nickel Plate RR was a big user of the 2-8-4, or 'Berkshire' type, especially for fast freights. Here one of its fleet simmers outside the NKP's Chicago roundhouse.

ABOVE: This is the original 'Superpower' series, a class of 2-8-4s supplied to the Boston and Albany RR in 1926. The large firebox carried by the four-wheel rear truck enabled high horsepower to be sustained. Other railroads, seeing the need for fast freights to beat highway competition, soon ordered similar locomotives.

RIGHT: The 2-10-4, or Texas, locomotive also provided high horsepower and was intended for the heavier trains. This example was built for the Chesapeake and Ohio RR, and is shown hauling coal to Lake Erie in 1943.

ABOVE: The Canadian Pacific's 'Royal Hudsons' were perhaps the most distinguished of the North American 4-6-4s introduced shortly before World War II. They hauled the most important passenger trains east of the Rockies. This 1957 picture shows one in charge of a Quebec train leaving Montreal's Windsor Street Station.

RIGHT: The 'Iosif Stalin' 2-8-4, introduced by Soviet Railroads in the 1930s, resembled US designs and appeared soon after Soviet railroad engineers had visited the US. The engineers were arrested on their return, and confined to a drawing office, owned by the secret police, until they had completed satisfactory designs for this 2-8-4 and a similar 2-10-2.

RIGHT: A French Railways 4-6-4 prototype. This is a 4-cylinder compound that appeared in 1949. With seven somewhat similar locomotives this machine hauled trains from Paris toward the Belgian frontier in the postwar period. Three of them were simples, and on test were 10 per cent less efficient than the compounds.

BELOW: British Railways had only one 4-6-4 tender locomotive, and that was by accident. This is LNER No.10000; it resembles one of the streamlined LNER Pacifics, but is in fact a rebuild of an unsuccessful high-pressure watertube-boiler prototype.

ABOVE: The American antecedents of the Soviet 'Iosif Stalin' 2-8-4 are evident in this close-up. The type appears to have been successful in the heavy passenger haulage for which it was intended, although manufacturing and raw material faults marred its first years. One of the type is preserved at Kiev, in Ukraine.

RIGHT: The five Hudsons built for the Canadian National's Toronto-Montreal service were reputedly the fastest locomotives in Canada, and one of them gained that country's speed record for steam traction. They had 80in driving wheels.

LEFT: Another view of the Canadian National's Hudson design. After the Toronto-Montreal trains became too heavy for these locomotives they were transferred to other services, including the Toronto-Windsor trains, which they worked until the end of the 1950s.

BOTTOM LEFT: This is one of the first batch of Canadian Pacific 4-6-4s, pulling out of Montreal on the dull Christmas Eve morning of 1958. The later 'Royal Hudsons' were almost identical, but with more advanced styling.

BELOW: From 1951 the 5ft 3in gauge Victorian Railways in Australia imported 70 R-Class Hudsons from Scotland. Their arrival coincided with the first of the diesels, so they had little chance to show what they could do. Several have been preserved, and haul frequent excursions.

128

LEFT: The final flowering of the New York Central's Hudson era is pictured in this publicity photograph of one of the streamlined members of the breed at the head of a new, re-equipped, '20th Century Limited.' Unlike earlier NYC Hudsons, this locomotive has disk driving wheels. In the 1930s, the NYC was still in hard-fought competition with the Pennsylvania RR for the first-class overnight New York-Chicago traffic. The four-track main line along the Hudson (also shown) was a theme of NYC's publicity about its 'Water-level Route.'

BELOW: The NYC was the first US railroad to adopt the 4-6-4 wheel arrangement, which is why the latter took the name 'Hudson.' Between 1927 and 1931 it bought over 200 of them, classed as J-1. They were ideal for the NYC's mainly flat routes and seemed never to be short of steam. This photograph shows five of them at the NYC terminal at La Salle St, Chicago, waiting to take out the several sections of the '20th Century Limited' on a peak-traffic evening, in the summer of 1929.

ABOVE LEFT: One of the celebrated LNER streamlined Pacifics at work for British Railways in the 1950s, hauling the 'Yorkshire Pullman' out of London. The stiff climb from the King's Cross terminal through damp tunnels was always a test of both locomotives and their crews. This class of locomotives, despite the careful maintenance required by its 3-cylinder layout, remained in service almost to the end of British steam traction in 1968.

LEFT: A side view of "Mallard," the most celebrated of the LNER streamliners. This locomotive holds the world steam record for steam traction of 126.5 mph. There have been other claims, but they have not been so well authenticated. The picture was made after "Mallard" had been restored to its original condition. Several other members of this class have been preserved, including one, "Dwight D Eisenhower," at Green Bay, Wisconsin.

ABOVE: The Southern Pacific preferred the 4-8-4 for its heavier passenger trains. This is one of the 'Daylight' series, so called because they hauled the Los Angeles-San Francisco 'Daylight' trains. They were introduced in 1937, had 80in driving wheels, and the unusually high boiler pressure of 300psi. Wartime variants had 73in wheels and were intended for more general duties.

LEFT: A somewhat run-down streamlined Pacific of the former LNER, "Quicksilver," hauls a London-Cambridge stopping train in 1955. The porthole in the tender shows that it has a narrow corridor giving access to the train, a device introduced between the wars to enable crews to be changed during long non-stop runs.

RIGHT: The GWR scorned streamlining, but to keep the critics quiet gave two of its locomotives a vaguely, and mildly absurd, streamlined trim. This picture was taken in 1935, and the trim was removed soon after.

BELOW: The LMS introduced its 'Coronation Scot' London-Glasgow train to match the streamliners of the LNER. The first streamlined Pacific built to haul it was itself named "Coronation." This picture shows one of the inaugural trains arriving at London's Euston Station in 1937.

MAIN PICTURE: The J Class of the Norfolk and Western RR were the last US streamliners in regular operation. In the 1950s they were responsible for hauling the two NW passenger trains between the eastern seaboard and Cincinnati. They were built in the NW's own workshops at Roanoke, Virginia, and the example illustrated still makes occasional excursions. With their roller bearings and careful balancing they were capable of high speeds, despite their relatively small driving wheels.

ABOVE: Another view of the Canadian National's streamlined 4-8-4. Five of these were built in Canada to haul Chicago-Toronto-Montreal trains over the Canadian sector, and five similar units were built in the US for CN's affiliate Grand Trunk Western, which handled the US sector. Avoidance of import duties was one factor in this arrangement.

TOP RIGHT: The four Victorian Railways Pacifics of class S were designed and built in Melbourne in 1928, and nine years later were streamlined to haul the new 'Spirit of Progress' between Melbourne and the New South Wales frontier at Albury. This is "Sir Thomas Mitchell" in 1947. The class remained in this service until diesels took over in 1951.

RIGHT: One of two streamlined Hudsons built for the German State Railway in 1935. One of them reached 124mph, and although this was slightly less than the record of "Mallard," the Germans claimed it was more meritorious, since it was not achieved with the help of a falling gradient.

"City of Wells," one of the light streamlined 'West Country' Pacifics designed by the Southern Railway in World War II.

TOP LEFT: The two streamlined locomotives on this page have certain outward similarities, and both were styled in the US. The upper picture shows one of the Indian Railways WP Pacifics, designed by Baldwin and supplied by many builders after World War II. This particular unit, shown hauling the 'Punjab Mail' out of Agra in 1963, was built by the Canadian Locomotive Company. Over 750 were built, the last batches being constructed in India during the 1960s.

BOTTOM LEFT: Mutton dressed as lamb. The locomotive beneath this streamlined exterior is of a United States Railroad Administration 4-8-2 design. The Norfolk and Western RR applied the streamlining so as to provide a small class of back-up locomotives to take over from the more modern J class streamliners whenever one of the latter became unavailable. It is shown on a stopping train at Blue Ridge, Virginia, in 1957.

LEFT: Part of the late afternoon Canadian Pacific commuter service at Montreal in 1957. Both large and small Pacifics are in use to haul these trains to the western suburbs and townships.

TOP: A WM 2-6-4 tank locomotive with a commuter train on the Eastern Railway in India, where every hour was peak hour. The picture dates from 1972, but the locomotive was imported from England in 1939.

ABOVE: A Fridays-only skiers' train to the northern townships awaits its passengers at Montreal in 1959, headed by one of the Canadian Pacific's 2-8-2 locomotives.

143

LEFT: Commuter trains at Madras, India, in 1972. The train on the left is hauled by a prewar British-built Pacific, while the purpose-built 2-8-4 tank locomotive was built in India in 1967.

BELOW: In the Paris eastern suburbs, a mainline train behind a 4-8-2 overtakes a commuter service hauled by a 2-6-2 tank of the former Est Railway.

RIGHT: One of the last steam commuter services in Europe was from the Gare du Nord in Paris, using modern 2-8-2 tank locomotives. There were 72 of these, which were claimed, probably for accounting reasons, to be conversions of older tender locomotives. They had rotary-cam valve gear and other refinements, and were attached to wooden-seated push-pull trains. This picture shows one of them leaving the terminus in 1969.

PREVIOUS PAGE: An 0-4-4 tank locomotive of the former London and South Western Railway passes the locomotive depot as it pulls out of Yeovil Town station in 1961. Several British companies in the late nineteenth century adopted this wheel arrangement for commuter-service locomotives. Later, as here, they were used on branch trains.

TOP LEFT: Another LSWR 0-4-4 tank locomotive, seen gathering passengers for a branchline service from Exeter in 1949.

TOP RIGHT: Fenchurch Street in east London was purely a commuter station and in the mid-1920s, as this picture shows, it was still served by trains of four-wheel stock. The locomotives are tank engines of the 2-4-2 and 0-6-0 wheel arrangements, built by the former Great Eastern Railway and carrying destination boards on their smokeboxes.

BOTTOM LEFT: The Caledonian Railway also built 0-4-4 tank locomotives for its many short-distance passenger services. By 1951, when this picture was taken, they had been superseded by bigger engines. This survivor had been relegated to the Highlands for yard service at Aviemore.

BOTTOM RIGHT: An M7 0-4-4 tank of the former LSWR at work for British Railways in Sussex. This class was introduced in 1897; one has been preserved at Steamtown in the US, and another at the National Railway Museum in York.

BELOW: One of the most successful tank locomotives for outer-suburban work was the taper-boiler 2-6-4 designed by William Stanier for the London Midland and Scottish Railway. Construction began in 1935, and a modified version was built after World War II. It had 69in driving wheels and two cylinders, although 37 of the several hundred built had three cylinders.

RIGHT: One of two fast 4-6-2 tank locomotives built by the London Brighton and South Coast Railway in 1912 for use on its 50-mile London-Brighton main line. With 80in driving wheels it was a fast runner. It is shown here on more humble duties for British Railways after electrification in the 1950s.

BOTTOM RIGHT: A predecessor of the LMS 2-6-4 tank illustrated opposite was the same company's parallel-boiler 2-6-4, which had similar dimensions to Stanier's design. The first were built in 1927, but this one was photographed with a suburban train at Birmingham in 1948.

LEFT: The Great Western Railway was so pleased with the 2-6-2 tank locomotive concept that it built several sizes. This is the smallest, introduced in 1904, and having driving wheels of only 49 inches. Only a handful were built, but they survived on branch lines until the 1950s.

BELOW LEFT: The New South Wales Government Railways preferred the 4-6-4 wheel arrangement for suburban tank locomotives. They ordered 145 between 1903 and 1917, mainly for Sydney services. Beyer Peacock of Manchester built the first examples, but the railway's Sydney workshops built 50. The center driving wheels were flangeless. This picture shows one of the last survivors leaving Newcastle in 1970.

ABOVE: Detroit was the last US city to enjoy a substantial steam-hauled commuter service. In its later years a variety of mainline locomotives were used. This is one of the streamlined 4-8-4 locomotives originally built for the US sector of the Montreal-Toronto-Chicago service, and relegated to commuter service when this picture was taken at the Detroit end of the line in 1958.

LEFT: Another of the Grand Trunk Western RR's commuter trains in 1958. This is the late afternoon service to Pontiac leaving Detroit, hauled by a 4-6-2 of a design by the World War I USRA (United States Railroad Administration). The USRA, to save resources in wartime, designed standard locomotives that any railroad could buy, and this light Pacific was one of the more popular choices.

BELOW: One of the last duties for this surviving Z.19 0-6-0 locomotive of the New South Wales Government Railways was yard work in the dock complex at Sydney. On working days in the early 1970s there were usually three or four present. Designed and mainly built by Beyer Peacock in the 1870s, the class was intended for mixed duties, but a 25mph speed limit was imposed as their riding was not perfect. They were characterized by closely-spaced second and third axles, which gave more space for the firebox.

RIGHT: Built for the Boston and Albany RR in 1916, this is a typical American yard engine. Wheels are small (51in) and closely spaced to ease passage over tight curves. Although a few companies moved to the 8-wheel switcher, Six-wheelers like this remained the favorite right up to the end of steam traction.

BELOW RIGHT: Another view of a NSWGR 4-6-4 commuter tank locomotive. This is tackling Fassifern Bank in 1970, with an evening train from the seaside suburb of Toronto to Newcastle. Many engines of this design were rebuilt as 4-6-0 tender locomotives after the Sydney electrifications.

ABOVE: The 'Dean Goods' 0-6-0 of the Great Western Railway was intended not just for freight, but for general duties. Introduced in 1883, it survived on lightly-laid lines until the 1950s. The picture shows one of the class leaving Brecon, in Central Wales.

LEFT: The resemblance of this locomotive to the 'Dean Goods' above is not accidental, because both have the same model of boiler and similar fittings. This 0-6-0 belonged to the Cambrian Railways and passed to the Great Western when the railways were amalgamated. It was then 'Great Westernized.'

ABOVE: The British maid-of-all-work, the 0-6-0, came in many shapes and sizes. This one was built for the London and South Western Railway and is shown in 1932 with a trainload of animals for the Bertram Mills Circus.

RIGHT: The Midland Railway did not favor freight locomotives bigger than the 0-6-0, although in the 1890s a locomotive shortage prompted it to buy some American-built 2-6-0s. This is an MR 0-6-0 in the 1950s, working a daily branch freight near Birmingham. The design dates from 1877, although the square firebox is a later modification.

MAIN PICTURE: This shows part of the second USTC 2-8-0 to return to Britain. After years of postwar service in Poland it was acquired by British railway enthusiasts and put to work on the Keighley and Worth Valley Railway.

INSET: The United States Transportation Corps 2-8-0 was a familiar sight on the British railways in 1942 and 1943, when these units, awaiting service with the armies in continental Europe, were put to good use hauling freight. They disappeared from Britain after the invasion of Normandy, but two returned. This inset shows one of them, which was retained by the Royal Engineers for training on the Longmoor Military Railway.

RIGHT: Hand coaling was common where labor was cheap and capital scarce. This picture was taken on the Indian meter gauge railways in the 1960s, but the practice could still be seen in the 1990s.

BELOW: The locomotive for the 'St Joaquin Daylight' is cleaned at the Southern Pacific's Bakersfield locomotive depot. This is a World War II publicity picture, showing how women were replacing men, but it also emphasizes the amount of work needed to keep a locomotive presentable.

ABOVE: Only at busy locomotive depots were powered turntables available, and hand-turning was the rule on short lines. Even when the turntable was in good order considerable labor was involved. Where land was cheap, as in North America, a Wye track layout was preferred. This picture shows a Mallet tank locomotive being turned on a French meter-gauge line.

RIGHT: After 1939 the British railways could never rely on supplies of the better grades of coal. Even in the 1960s the kind of slack and small coal shown in this picture was supplied for mainline runs. This is a Pacific at Salisbury crew-changing point on the London-Exeter line, and the incoming crew is giving a hand to the outgoing by shovelling coal from the back of the tender closer to the footplate.

LEFT: One of the massive postwar 4-8-4s of Spanish National Railways pulls out of Zaragoza in 1969. These 5ft 6in gauge locomotives were built for heavy haulage over some of the hilly inter-city routes in Spain. However, their 75in driving wheels allowed fast running, too.

BOTTOM LEFT: The last masterpiece of the French engineer Andre Chapelon was his 242A.1, a prototype 4-8-4 embodying all his technical improvements, including a triple chimney. Although this postwar locomotive produced a better performance than the existing electric locomotives, French National Railways' choice of extensive electrification meant that this design was not put into production.

BELOW: This 4-8-4 of the South African Railways was one of a class fitted with condensers, for service in arid areas. The grilles at the side of the tender can be seen, as can the pipe carrying exhaust steam to the condenser elements in the tender.

LEFT: A wartime publicity picture featuring the Southern Pacific 'Daylight' 4-8-4. This unit was built in 1943, and following batches had 73in driving wheels instead of 80in. This was to give them a better performance as fast freight haulers, although the earlier series, also described as a general purpose design, was often used for freight as well as for the haulage of crack trains like the 'Sunset Limited' and the 'Daylights.'

BELOW: The New York Central called its 4-8-4 type, 'Niagaras.' Built from 1945 as general service locomotives they hauled many of the NYC's celebrated trains. They achieved very high monthly mileages but nevertheless were replaced by diesels in the 1950s.

ABOVE: The 4-8-4 was first adopted by the Great Northern RR, hence the name 'Northern.' The GN's competitor the Milwaukee RR also bought it and one of the Milwaukee units is shown here as it prepares to start a freight for the Pacific coast out of its Illinois terminal of Bensonville. Between 1927 and World War II about a thousand 4-8-4s were built for US railroads; it was probably the most useful of the 'superpower' types.

RIGHT: This class of Santa Fe RR 4-8-4 had a device that could raise the chimney to improve the draft for the fire, and lower it to clear overhead structures.

BELOW: With its main lines over the prairies, the Chicago Burlington and Quincy RR could make good use of high-horsepower 4-8-4s like this, especially for the faster freights. Some railroads used the type only for freight, and a few for passenger trains only, but most treated it as a general duties locomotive.

RIGHT: The last US-built 4-8-4s to remain in service were the 56 supplied by Baldwin and Alco to the Mexican National Railroad in 1946. First used in passenger service, they ended their days on freight. This example is shown hauling a freight out of Mexico City in 1961.

BELOW RIGHT: Between 1937 and 1944 the Union Pacific RR received 45 of these big 4-8-4s for use on its best passenger services. This one at Grand Island, Nebraska, was of the second batch, which had 80in instead of 77in driving wheels. The final batch had double chimneys. On test, one reached 102 mph.

BELOW: The postwar passenger locomotive of Soviet Railways was this light 4-8-4, which replaced 2-6-2s on some of the main lines, including the busy Moscow-Leningrad route. This picture shows one of the class entering Leningrad with a headboard announcing that it is a special train carrying a Polish delegation.

BOTTOM: A general service 4-8-4 of the Southern Pacific RR. This batch, delivered in 1930, was later developed into the 'Daylight' class.

ABOVE: The 4-8-4 became almost a symbol of rebirth in the 1920s, when the Canadian National began to order the type to replace the variegated collection of locomotives it had received from its impecunious constituent companies. This is one of the final series, photographed at Toronto in 1957 on the final day of regular steam haulage of the Toronto-Montreal trains.

RIGHT: After their relegation from the better passenger trains, the CN 4-8-4s continued to run between Toronto and Montreal on freights and extra workings. Here No.6237 has its fire cleaned at the Turcot locomotive depot in Montreal in 1958.

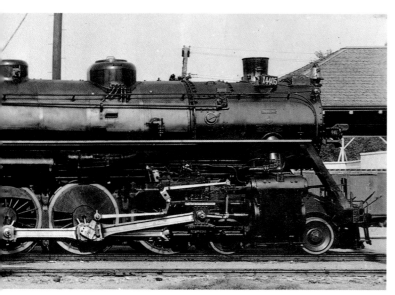

PREVIOUS PAGE (INSET): Another view of the Soviet Railways P36 4-8-4. This example has been preserved in working order. (MAIN PICTURE): British-built lightweight 4-8-2 locomotives at Oudtshoorn locomotive depot in South Africa in 1970.

ABOVE: A 4-8-2 locomotive built by Alco for the Illinois Central RR. The 4-8-2 was known as the 'Mountain' type and was seen mostly in America, although France built some fine examples.

LEFT: The 4-8-2 lost favor when the 2-8-4 and 4-8-4 appeared, but some railroads liked it. This Canadian National design was the final development of the type. Painted apple green and streamlined in spirit, if not in substance, 6076 steams out of Toronto Union Station in 1957.

RIGHT: An earlier design of Canadian National 4-8-2, also at Toronto in 1957.

ABOVE: When the London Midland and Scottish Railway renewed its motive power in the 1930s it introduced this 2-8-0 design to replace the rough-riding 0-8-0s it had inherited from its constituent companies. Known as the 8F, it was a freight version of the very successful Class 5 4-6-0. Hundreds were built, and during World War II several railways built them in their workshops. Some were sent abroad, and a few were still working in Turkey in the 1980s. The picture shows one on a freight service in 1968, steam's last year on British Railways.

RIGHT: Although the Midland Railway used small 0-6-0 designs for its freight trains, its Derby workshops did build some 2-8-0s like this one. The design was intended for the Somerset and Dorset Joint Railway, in which the Midland had a half-share. This line passed over the Mendips south of Bath, and its gradients were too much for 0-6-0s. The picture shows one of the preserved units, painted in the colors of the LMS, which took over the Midland's interest in the SDJR after the railway amalgamation of 1922.

TOP LEFT: The 141R 2-8-2 of French National Railways was designed and built in America with French participation. Intended as the basic locomotive for the war-torn French railways in 1945, it was unlike prewar French locomotives in its simplicity and ruggedness. It was a 2-cylinder simple, and hundreds were built for passenger and freight operations, many surviving right up to the end of steam in France.

TOP RIGHT: Another postwar French design, built in France, was the 241P 4-8-2. It was a small class, and in the 1950s and 1960s it was switched from route to route as electrification progressed. This 1969 picture shows one being coaled at Chaumont after working a passenger train in the Paris-Basle service.

CENTER RIGHT: This is a French 2-8-2 of prewar design. A compound locomotive, it is far more sophisticated than the 141R illustrated opposite. In compensation for its higher maintenance costs, this 141P class was probably the world's most effective steam locomotive in terms of horsepower per ton. When photographed in 1953 it was handling long-distance trains between Paris and Britanny.

BOTTOM LEFT: An Australian 4-8-2 of the 1930s. The 25 members of this New South Wales Class 57 heavy freight locomotive had three cylinders, with the British Gresley's 'conjugated' valve gear. Their single-piece frames were cast in the US, where this technique had been introduced. Unusually for Australian locomotives, they also had a mechanical stoker.

BOTTOM RIGHT: Another of the French 241P type, about to take over from a diesel at Chaumont. Thirty-five of these 4-cylinder compounds were built, the design being partly based on a prototype of 1930. It had 79in driving wheels.

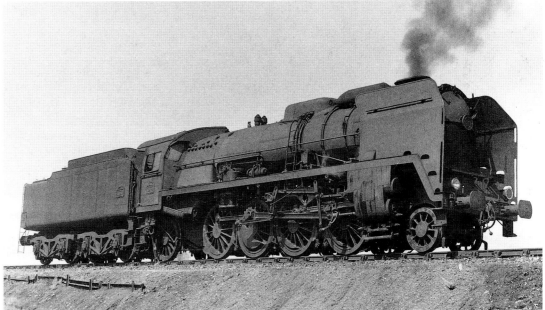

TOP LEFT: On many North American railroads the 2-8-2, or Mikado, became a maid-of-all-work (rather like the 0-6-0 in Britain), although when it first appeared in 1911 it was regarded as a freight hauler. This is one of a class built for the Northern Pacific RR.

TOP RIGHT: Very different from the North American 2-8-2 was the 100-strong D52 class of the Indonesian National Railways. Built in Germany by Krupp in the 1950s, it became the basic mainline freight and passenger locomotive. This member of the class was photographed in 1972 as it was turned by a band of paid and unpaid labor.

CENTER LEFT: By the 1950s, North American Mikados were used mainly on secondary freight trains. Here is a Canadian National example, approaching Montreal in 1957 with a train of merchandise.

BOTTOM LEFT: By the 1950s the North American 2-8-0 was largely employed on branches and on short-distance freights. This Canadian Pacific 2-8-0 has had steam momentarily cut off after a bout of wheel-slip as it restarts its train at Toronto.

BOTTOM RIGHT: A New South Wales Government Railways 2-8-2 slips off the turntable at Broadmeadow. Twenty of these oil-burning Mikado engines were acquired from Baldwin-Lima-Hamilton in the US in 1952. They were later converted to coal-burners. They lasted until 1972, and four have been preserved.

LEFT: The British wartime Ministry of Supply during World War II designed and ordered hundreds of 'Austerity' 2-8-0 locomotives. These were intended mainly for service in Europe as the armies advanced. After World War II some stayed in continental Europe and others were used by British Railways. This example was an exception, being allocated to a Royal Engineers training railway.

LEFT: A Baldwin Locomotive Works publicity picture of 1920, showing a massive delivery of 2-10-2 locomotives to the Southern Pacific RR. Samuel Vauclain, Baldwin's president, stands in the foreground.

RIGHT: Very few 2-10-2 locomotives were built for Canadian railways, but the CNR used this design for some heavy freight services. The picture dates from 1957 and was taken at Winnipeg.

BELOW: One of the last US 2-10-2s in service, this locomotive hauls a Bolivian State Railroad passenger train in 1968. One of this class, built by Baldwin in 1942, still survives in Bolivia in the early 1990s.

ABOVE: From 1912, the French Nord Railway used the 2-10-0 for its coal trains. It was a 4-cylinder compound, and one of the early series is seen here on the right. The other locomotive is the postwar French National Railways 2-10-0 which was used for the same traffic.

BELOW: The Norfolk and Western RR was primarily a coal-hauler and used Mallet locomotives, often double-headed, for taking West Virginian coal down to tidewater. The NW railroad town of Roanoke witnessed scenes like this up to the end of the 1950s. The nearest locomotive has since been preserved, and hauls passenger excursions most years.

RIGHT: British Railways finally built a class of 2-10-0s and one, "Evening Star," was so named because it was the last steam locomotive built for the British railways. Here it is seen on an excursion train in the 1980s.

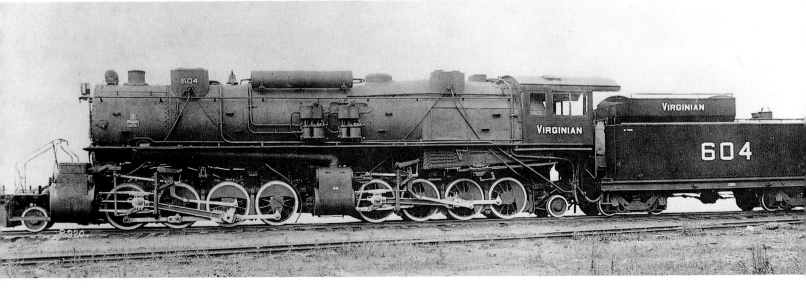

TOP LEFT: A Norfolk and Western Mallet pushing a coal train over Blue Ridge, Virginia. This is a compound Mallet, as indicated by the bigger diameter of the low-pressure cylinder at the front.

TOP RIGHT: A New South Wales Government Railways Garratt is washed down at its depot. These 4-8-4 + 4-8-4 locomotives were imported from Manchester in 1952-57 for heavy coal and grain trains. They weighed 265 tons, but their axleload was only 16 tons. Apart from a one-off Garratt built for Soviet Railroads, these were the biggest locomotives ever built in Britain, and several have been preserved.

CENTER LEFT: The Garratt was a British concept for an articulated locomotive, with one boiler suspended between two pivoted engine units. It was widely used in the British Commonwealth, and this 2ft gauge example in South Africa is still running in Natal.

BOTTOM LEFT: Compared to later US Mallets, this 2-8-8-2, built for the Virginian RR in 1912, was quite small.

BOTTOM RIGHT: A close-up of the leading engine unit of a Norfolk and Western Mallet. The rear engine cylinder, just visible, is the same diameter as the forward cylinder, indicating that this 4-6-6-4 is a simple-expansion locomotive.

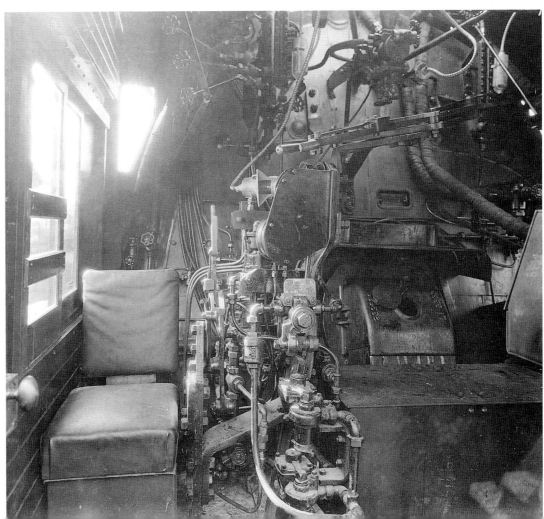

ABOVE: Generally regarded as the biggest steam locomotives ever built, the 'Big Boy' 4-8-8-4 Mallets of the Union Pacific RR weighed 595 tons. They were designed to haul 3600-ton freights up the rising main line into the Rockies.

ABOVE RIGHT: Sometimes the pumps for the air brakes were placed on the smokebox door, as on this Baltimore and Ohio RR 2-6-6-2 Mallet of 1931.

LEFT: The Southern Pacific, which had mountain tunnels, introduced Mallet locomotives with forward cabs to avoid suffocation of crews by smoke and steam.

RIGHT: The reversed, but forward-looking, seat in a SP cab-in-front locomotive. The pipework demonstrates the complexity of the later steam locomotives.

LEFT: Among named trains the London-Paris 'Golden Arrow' Pullman was unusual in that it was two trains, separated by 21 miles of water. This is the southbound French train in 1953, headed by a compound Pacific of the 231E class.

BELOW: The corresponding British 'Golden Arrow' is seen leaving London's Victoria Station for the port of Dover in 1947, hauled by a 'West Country' Pacific.

LEFT: The 'Cheltenham Spa Express,' popularly known as the 'Cheltenham Flyer' and for some years the world's fastest train, prepares for a record run in 1923. The Great Western 2-cylinder 4-6-0 is called "Saint Bartholomew."

ABOVE: In the 1920s one of the best Southern Pacific named trains was the Chicago-Los Angeles 'Golden State Limited' which made the run in 61 hours. The Rock Island RR handled it over the eastern sector into Chicago. It is shown here behind a 4-8-2; the SP had not yet invested in the 4-8-4.

RIGHT: The Santa Fe RR's 'Grand Canyon Express' passes a side-tracked freight. The 3765 class 4-8-4s were made by Baldwin from 1938, and had 300psi boiler pressure. Driving wheels were 80in, and the design was well-balanced, enabling 90mph to be achieved without strain. After diesels took over the fast passenger runs, this class was very successful with the California fruit trains. Trains of 100 refrigerator cars were sometimes pulled at 80mph behind these locomotives.

ABOVE: The Snowdon Mountain Railway in North Wales has operated with steam traction for a hundred years. The locomotive here is an 0-4-2 tank built in 1923 by the Swiss Locomotive Company: Switzerland being the most experienced user of mountain-climbing rack railways. The gauge of this railway is unusual, 2ft 7½in.

LEFT: A narrow gauge (2ft 6in) line that has been converted to standard gauge since the picture was taken in 1960. In Bosnia, the Dubrovnik-Sarajevo train climbs through the mountains behind a 2-8-2 and 0-8-2.

RIGHT: The narrow-gauge Tallylyn Railway in Wales was faltering in the 1950s, but was then rescued by railway enthusiasts. The locomotive "Douglas" is an 0-4-0 well tank built in 1918 and obtained from another narrow-gauge railway.

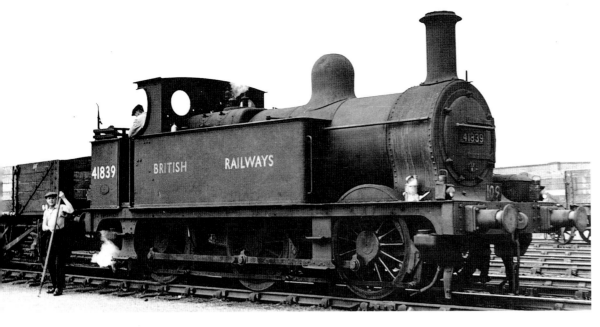

TOP LEFT: In Britain the 0-6-0 tank locomotive was the favorite for yard work. This is a 19th century design, and the rudimentary cab will be noted. It was built by the Midland Railway and eventually became part of the British Railways stock.

TOP RIGHT: In North America some companies used the 0-8-0 yard locomotive. This is an example owned by the Canadian National. Such locomotives were also used for short-trip workings.

CENTER LEFT: The Great Western Railway favored this type 0-6-0 tank locomotive, which it termed 'pannier tank.' The locomotive shown here was built by British Railways to GWR design soon after nationalization. It was a lightweight version of the GWR standard pannier tank, weighing only 42 tons and having 49in wheels. The yardsmen standing behind the locomotive have their standard-issue shunting poles, with which they engaged and disengaged the three-link couplings used on British freight cars.

BOTTOM LEFT: Night operations at the big Southern Railway yard at Feltham, near London. The locomotives are 0-8-0 tanks, of which a small class of eight units had been introduced in 1929 specifically for yard work.

BOTTOM RIGHT: The United States Railroad Administration in World War I took the bold step of designing a standard 0-8-0 switcher for the US companies. At that time few railroads believed they had a need for it, but in the following decade many companies did buy it. This was one of the first, built for the New York Central in 1918.

ABOVE: After World War II several new types of 2-6-0 appeared in Britain, as replacements for old 0-6-0s. This is the Class K1, designed by the LNER, of which 70 units were built from 1949. Unlike prewar LNER 2-6-0s, it had two cylinders, not three, partly because in postwar conditions the careful maintenance required by the 3-cylinder layout could not be guaranteed.

BELOW: The American 2-6-0, or 'Mogul,' appeared much earlier than the British one and, partly for this reason, it was less refined than the British examples. It found a useful role on branch lines after it had been superseded by larger types on the main lines, and some units survived in Canada until the late 1950s.

RIGHT: This truly modern 2-6-0 was produced by British Railways in 1953, and 65 were built. This one has been preserved in running order. Two larger designs of 2-6-0 were also built by BR.

RIGHT: The Great Western Railway had been building Moguls since before World War I, when this type was among the designs incorporating some US features adopted as GWR standards. This locomotive is hauling a secondary passenger train in Wales in 1950, but the type was used on all kinds of duties, from fast passenger to slow freight.

LEFT: A seemingly tiny 2-6-0 of Canadian Pacific takes the Waltham branch train out of Ottawa in 1957.

RIGHT: The Canadian National's locomotive depot at Toronto in 1957. A Pacific stands in the foreground, ready for dispatch, while an 0-8-0 switches odd cars in the background.

BELOW LEFT: A line-up of South African locomotives at the Bloemfontein depot in 1970. The second from the right is a US-built 4-6-2.

BELOW RIGHT: A Scottish locomotive depot in the 1950s. This is St. Margarets, Edinburgh, with an LNER 2-6-0 passing on the main line.

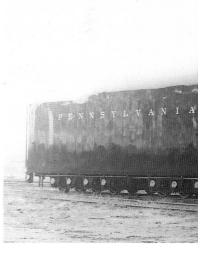

TOP RIGHT: As electric and diesel traction increasingly challenged steam, efforts were made to depart from the conventional Stephenson steam locomotive. One possible technology, which had had a moderate success in Sweden, was to replace cylinders and pistons with turbines, suitably geared to the driving wheels. A British turbomotive 4-6-2 operated on the LMS for some years from 1935. Much larger was this 6-8-6 built for the Pennsylvania RR in 1944, which had a 6000 hp main and 1500 hp reverse turbine. Like the LMS example, it worked quite well but, being a novel prototype, had high maintenance costs. It was abandoned in 1949.

CENTER RIGHT: Another route to change was the steam-turbine-electric, in which the steam drove a turbine that powered a generator whose electricity was fed to traction motors. The Norfolk and Western built one of these, and the Chesapeake and Ohio built three in 1947. The NW unit worked well and was used as a pusher over Blue Ridge, whereas the CO units never really survived their teething troubles. The NW version did at least prove that the idea was viable and, with a different ratio between the prices of diesel oil and coal, it might have justified itself.

ABOVE: A French locomotive depot. This is Tours in 1954, with the 231G 4-cylinder compound Pacifics which at that time were handling the main passenger trains in that area.

BOTTOM RIGHT: As locomotives got bigger, the moving components like connecting and coupling rods became heavier, and their rapid movement set up great stresses. Some engineers favored dividing the power between several sets of wheels, so these components would not need to cope with so much thrust. On the Pennsylvania RR from 1942 two classes of such divided-drive locomotives appeared, the T1 4-4-4-4 of which 52 were built, and the Q2 4-4-6-4 totaling 26. The T1 was for passenger and the Q2 for general duties. They were quite successful, although the Q2 had high fuel consumption. They were capable of very powerful performance, but little useful work could be found for them after diesels had taken over the most difficult assignments.

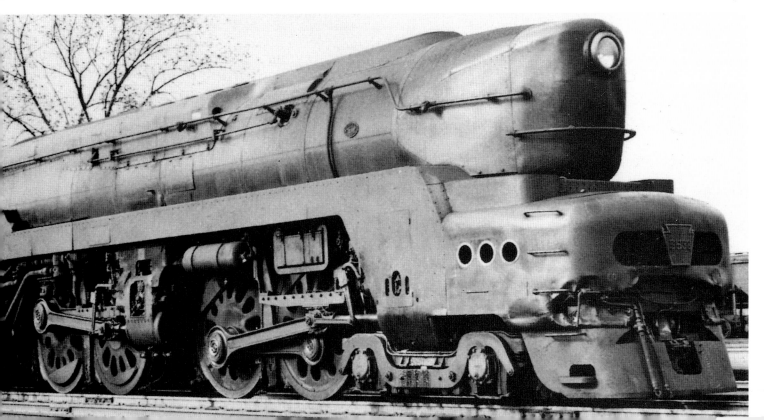

THE MODERN ERA

By 1980, most of the world's rail systems had abandoned steam traction but, because India and China were among the countries still using it, there were several thousand steam locomotives in regular service. Both these countries had dieselization and electrification schemes, but both also planned to maintain steam traction into the twenty-first century.

They had good reasons for doing so. Electric traction is cheaper than steam only on intensively-used or steeply-graded routes, while diesel traction, although cheaper and more convenient to operate than steam, places demands on mechanical and electrical industries that may already be overwhelmed with orders from other branches of the economy. Both countries have ample coal resources but little oil. Both possess massive workforces skilled in the use and maintenance of steam locomotives, while graduates from electrical and diesel technology schools are urgently needed elsewhere.

Both India and China have electrified some exceptionally busy lines, and completely dieselized a few more, and there has been a tendency to dieselize the faster long-distance passenger trains. But in both countries a high proportion of the freight tonnage is still hauled behind steam, and both have a standard heavy freight locomotive that is used almost exclusively in this service: in China the massively-built QJ 2-10-2, a Chinese version of a Russian design, and in India the WG 2-8-2, very British-looking but incorporating American features.

By the end of the 1980s steam traction was clearly on the way out in South Africa and Indonesia, but it seemed likely to survive some more years in southern Africa. In South Africa itself, withdrawn mainline steam locomotives have found work on industrial lines, and in neighboring Zimbabwe Garratt-type locomotives are still in use. Zimbabwe, like several other ex-colonial countries, discovered

LEFT: WG type 2-8-2s of India's Western Railway wait in the coaling line. About 2500 of these 5ft 6in gauge freight units were built in the postwar years and most are still in service. The first batch was built in Britain, but most were turned out by India's Chittaranjan Locomotive Works.

BOTTOM LEFT: A big Chinese freight yard at Kharbin, in Manchuria. To the left, tracks lead down from the hump into reception lines. Several standard 2-10-2 locomotives can be seen.

ABOVE: Toward the end of mainline steam traction in Indonesia a 90-year-old Scottish-built 2-4-0 moves a modern Krupp-built 2-8-2 around the main works at Madiun. A Swiss-built Mallet 2-6-6-0 of 1927 awaits its turn.

CENTER RIGHT: In eastern Germany the World War II 'Kriegslok' 2-10-0 could still be seen working in the early 1990s. This one is hauling a freight through Dresden.

BOTTOM RIGHT: This is a meter-gauge 4-6-0 at Varanasi (Benares) in India. Apart from the commodious cab, it is a typically British 4-6-0. Many British locomotive building companies shared the Indian orders, but had to follow standard Indian designs. However, this P class locomotive was built in India at the Ajmer Works in about 1914.

TOP: Fitters take time off for a photograph at a Sumatran locomotive depot. Shown are a pair of 2-8-0s of a type supplied by German makers to the Dutch East Indian State Railways in 1914.

ABOVE: An Indonesian local train stops for passengers in a main street. The locomotive is a 4-4-0 built in Germany in 1914.

that dieselization brought more problems than it solved, not the least being the high cost of imported spare parts and the disappointing gap between the diesel's high utilization potential and the mileage between repairs that was achieved in practice. In Indonesia, steam can still be found in the canefields.

In Europe, in the early 1990s there were a few pockets of steam traction in Poland and in Hungary, and in the former Soviet Union a steam locomotive could occasionally be seen replacing an absent diesel in freight yards or on short-distance trains. Steam had long survived in eastern Germany, but by 1992 it was limited to a number of narrow-gauge lines, where it was expected to continue if only for touristic reasons. In South America there were still a few steam lines, especially in Argentina, while Bolivia was the last workplace of the American 2-10-2. The heavy-duty narrow-gauge Rio Turbio Railroad in Patagonia was steam operated, although falling demand for the coal which it carried meant that few trains were running in the early 1990s.

Canefield and forestry lines, almost always narrow-gauge, sometimes persisted with steam traction. In Romania, where standard-gauge steam traction was at a virtual end by 1992, there are still some narrow-gauge forestry lines under steam. The same is true of the Philippines, while in Cuba the peak of the sugar season still witnesses scores of American-built steam locomotives emerging from their sheds to work hard for a few months.

While conventional steam operation was disappearing from the world's railroads, the aesthetic and sentimental appeal of steam locomotion ensured that it would live on in other ways. Rudimentary railroad museums had long existed, but the disappearance from daily view of the steam train gave impetus to the enlargement of existing, and the establishment of new, museums centered on retired steam locomotives. In Britain and several other European countries, it proved possible to create national railroad museums, and the British National Railway Museum at York became the world's biggest. In larger countries like the US and Australia, railroad museums tended to be established on a state basis, usually privately funded but often with state support. Pennsylvania and California, in particular, established impressive museums, as did the Australian states.

Some of the bigger museums were able to offer the

sight of a steam locomotive moving under its own steam, emphasizing that the appeal of the locomotive was precisely in its motion, and that static exhibits might interest specialists but would not attract a mass audience for more than a few minutes. The sight, smell, and sound of a steam locomotive in action, combined with nostalgia and curiosity about the past, was the main attraction of the steam tourist railroad, which appeared in the 1950s and was flourishing in many countries by the 1970s.

The Talyllyn Railway in Wales marked a turning point in the early 1950s. It was a defunct narrow-gauge line and was re-opened through the efforts of railway enthusiasts anxious to preserve not so much steam traction, but the whole railroad and the atmosphere it created. The success of this venture encouraged other enthusiast groups in Britain, and in the 1960s the standard-gauge Bluebell Line was established in southern England. With the success of this, the enthusiast-operated steam railroad movement took off, and new lines are still being established all over the world.

Among the earlier US steam tourist railroads was the Strasburg, which has its terminal in an advantageous position alongside the Pennsylvania Railroad Museum and benefits from its location in a tourist area. Proximity to large cities, or to tourist areas, is of great help. The cities not only provide customers but also the steady flow of enthusiast part-time workers that most of these lines need in order to survive. The several Welsh narrow-gauge lines, and the three-foot (910mm) gauge lines in the Rockies, present fine scenery to their passengers and would probably not have survived without it.

One of the more painful lessons absorbed by successive enthusiast-run lines is that railroad fans themselves do not provide a sufficient clientele. Like it or not, these railroads have to obtain revenue by attracting ordinary families. In America, this sometimes means laying on Wild West scenes that can be painfully-absurd to the serious enthusiast, and in Britain there is a less controversial echo in the 'Santa specials' that many lines operate over the Christmas holiday period.

A few tourist lines are quite long, and in Britain there is a stretch of a one-time main line, the Great Central Railway, that is used for running steam trains. But, on the whole, the preserved lines offer a nostalgic glimpse of what railroad travel was like on secondary and branch lines. Yet steam traction in its glory was seen above all in the mainline fast passenger train, and to resurrect this kind of service it is necessary to use trackage still in regular use. This means that the approval of railroad managements is required and this may, or may not, be forthcoming. In Australia and South Africa, managements are generally keen supporters of steam excursion trains, and some Australian state railroads run their own 'vintage trains' for publicity purposes, as well as allowing responsible enthusiast organizations to run their own trains at weekends. The same is generally true of France and Germany, although France suffers from a lack of suitable locomotives, too many having been scrapped in the period between the end of steam and the realization that steam locomotives might still have a future.

In the US and Britain, mainline steam excursions seemed secure by the early 1990s, but if the past is any guide they will not have a smooth ride. Since the goodwill of railroad management is so essential, their fate could depend on purely personal factors. For a long period after the end of steam in Britain, British Rail's management were opposed to steam excursions, largely in the belief that the appearance of a steam locomotive would dissipate the progressive image that BR believed it had gained by abolishing the steam locomotive. But then there came a change of heart and soon BR was not only offering a few specific routes to enthusiast steam operators but had also instituted its own-brand steam trains on a frequent-running basis, including a regular steam-hauled trip from London to the popular tourist destination of Stratford-on-Avon.

British Rail nevertheless sometimes made things difficult by imposing conditions. However, such conditions, though arguable, were understandable. BR's insistence on modern standards, for example, prevented the operation of vintage coaches on its lines. In New South Wales, after a regular train ran into the back of a steam excursion, resulting in fatalities, restrictions were imposed. In the US, impossibly high insurance requirements forced the cancellation of some excursions.

LEFT: The British 0-6-0 lived on into the 1990s in India and Pakistan. Here one of that numerous breed busies itself as station pilot at Patna on India's Eastern Railway. The heavy freight traffic now carried by Indian Railways is well portrayed in this picture.

RIGHT: Many of the LMS Railway's class 5 4-6-0s have been preserved, partly because they are a useful type for private steam operations, and partly because so many were available.

In the US, it was the personal factor that was dominant, with some managements hostile and others welcoming. It was not always a question of personalities, however. Some railroads were so busy that a steam excursion could only disrupt regular scheduled trains. Others were, for one reason or another, so desperate to polish their local image that they welcomed a public relations gesture like the operation of a steam train. Because there were so many US companies, there was rarely a problem finding a hospitable railroad. In the early 1990s some railroads were highly sympathetic. The Norfolk Southern RR, heir to the last big steam-operated railroad (Norfolk and Western), was enthusiastically supporting trips by two of its retired locomotives, a Mallet and a streamlined 4-8-4. In the west, the Union Pacific was a willing host to excursions hauled by a UP Mallet or a UP 4-8-4.

Railroad administrations in other countries followed these examples. The New Zealand Government Railways had been among the pioneers when they organized the 'Kingston Flyer,' and in the 1990s the 'Kingston Flyer' was still available, although not regularly scheduled. Indonesia, Sri Lanka and a few other countries maintained steam locomotives that could be used to haul chartered trains. Even Russia was organizing what it called 'retrotrains' composed of vintage rolling stock hauled over some sections by steam locomotives.

In Russia, and a few other countries, it is recognized that tourist railroads and steam excursions are not only good for the tourist trade but might also become sources of hard currency. The Chinese state travel agency organizes tours for foreign railroad enthusiasts and, because steam traction is extensively used as a matter of course, does not need to

LEFT: Steam locomotive construction in China continued into the 1990s. A pair of 2-8-2s nears completion in the Tangshan Works. This type was favored by Chinese industrial lines.

BELOW RIGHT: A 2-8-0 stands at Grand Canyon, awaiting returning passengers. The Grand Canyon RR, once the Grand Canyon branch of the Santa Fe RR, extends 64 miles and is one of the more recent US tourist railroads.

BELOW: A Baldwin 2-8-0 handles the afternoon service of the Sierra RR in California.

operate special steam excursions. The Russians have begun to take railroad museums seriously, and they also provide some steam excursion trains. One problem is that under the Soviet regime there had been successive scrap metal drives that devoured examples of the earlier types of Russian locomotive. Even locomotives earmarked for preservation were hauled off to the scrapyards. The result is that there is an impressive number of steam locomotives preserved in Russia, but almost all are of the few classes built since 1925.

In other countries, too, it was the designs last in service that provided the bulk of the preserved locomotives. In Britain the GWR was the favorite among preservationists, and nine of its 30-strong 'Manor' class 4-6-0s were preserved. In New South Wales, where colliery lines used steam for some years after the end of mainline steam, the entire fleet of 2-8-2 tank locomotives used by the South Maitland Railway was saved from the torch, 14 units in all. In the US, this duplication of preserved designs did not happen, mainly because there were so many classes to choose from and the best-known or best-loved had been mostly scrapped before the possibilities of preservation had become clear. A number of US tourist lines secured locomotives from Canadian railroads, where dieselization occured later, while one or two entirely new locomotives (standard American-style 2-8-2s) were imported from China, where steam locomotive construction continued into the 1990s.

In almost all countries industrial railroads operated steam locomotives long after mainline steam had disappeared. In Britain there were still 700 industrial steam locomotives operating in 1970. Although these have now been replaced, it is not unknown for a diesel yard engine undergoing repair to be relieved by a resurrected steam locomotive. In Bristol, a coal contractor in this situation actually borrowed a preserved steam locomotive for a few weeks. Industrial steam locomotives are working in eastern Europe, and in Germany the Aachen coal mines still witness steam operations. Though the 'golden age' of steam may be long gone, examples of many types, both working and preserved, can still be found around the world.

BELOW: Steam traction at Concepcion, Chile. This city had a perpetual haze, thanks to the soft local coal burned by these locomotives. The 4-8-2 on the left is essentially of Baldwin design, but was built in Japan in the 1950s. The US and Japanese 4-8-2s were the biggest locomotives on the Chilean 5ft 6in gauge lines. Smaller locomotives came from Scotland and Germany. The locomotive in the right background is a 2-6-0 built by Henschel in 1912.

BELOW: The grass-grown main line of the Paraguay National Railroad is gently trodden by a Baldwin 2-8-0 of 1906. This locomotive was obtained second-hand from the Argentinian State Railroad, although most trains were, and are, hauled by British-built 2-6-0s. This railroad has been moribund for decades, but somehow has always kept going. Its locomotives are woodburners, but from time to time grandiose plans are unveiled for dieselization, or even electrification. Train service is sparse. The only regular service is a train that covers the full length of the line from the capital, Asuncion, to the Argentine frontier at Encarnacion, and this only runs twice or three times weekly.

The preserved "Lord Nelson"
4-6-0 of Britain's Southern
Railway heads an excursion
in northern England.

BELOW: A 4-8-0 of the former Buenos Aires Great Southern Railway. The broad-gauge 4-8-0 was used by this company in several variants, and was especially useful for the many fast freights operated by the railroad, which had a seasonal fruit traffic. This locomotive, which has three cylinders, was built by Armstrong Whitworth in England in 1929. In the 1950s the class was refurbished. It hauled not only freight but also long-distance sleeping-car trains.

RIGHT: The daily passenger service of the Cuzco-Santa Ana Railroad, of Peru zigzags out of Cuzco behind a German-built postwar 2-8-2. This 3ft gauge line serves the ancient settlement of Macchu Pichu, and therefore has a considerable tourist traffic.

BELOW RIGHT: On the same railroad an Alco 2-8-2 of 1920 climbs above Cuzco with a freight train. This line was largely dieselized by the 1980s, but steam traction was retained as a back-up and for possible excursion use. The other well-known Peruvian 3ft gauge line, the Huancayo-Huancavellica Railroad retained steam traction into the late 1980s and then kept steam locomotives available for excursions.

TOP LEFT: In California the Southern Pacific's steam-hauled 'Daylight' streamliners were an early victim of dieselization, but the refurbishment of a 'Daylight' 4-8-4 has enabled a close approximation of these trains to be operated from time to time, as shown here.

TOP RIGHT: Another view of the Grand Canyon RR. The original Santa Fe line, and now the present line, deliver passengers to within a few yards of the edge. In the early 1990s the RR was operating one return service daily from Williams, an Arizona tourist center, giving passengers several hours at the Canyon. The locomotive is an Alco 2-8-0 of 1906, formerly belonging to the Lake Superior and Ishpeming RR.

BOTTOM LEFT: Union Pacific 4-8-4 No. 844, renumbered 8444, has been a frequent performer on US excursion trains. It is shown here returning to its home base after attending the 1984 New Orleans Fair.

BOTTOM RIGHT: Another view of the Cuzco-Santa Ana Railroad in Peru. An Alco 2-8-2 built in 1926 switches a modern passenger coach at the Cuzco terminal. In its final steam days, this railroad had three US-built 2-8-2s, a Baldwin 4-6-0, and a German 2-8-2. A Japanese diesel locomotive was acquired in the 1960s, along with some railcars.

Chinese QJ 2-10-2s at work
in Manchuria.

INSET: Work in progress at the Changchun locomotive depot in Manchuria. The locomotive is a QJ 2-10-2, the standard Chinese freight locomotive.

MAIN PICTURE: Another view of Chinese QJ 2-10-2 locomotives at Changchun in 1988.

ABOVE: Beyer Peacock 2-8-2 tank locomotives working on the South Maitland colliery line in New South Wales.

LEFT: One of the many Chinese narrow-gauge forestry lines. Behind the first two vehicles, invisible in the picture, is a long line of empty bolster trucks, used for transporting tree trunks. The passenger car was used earlier in the day for a party of British railway enthusiasts.

RIGHT: Another industrial railroad. This is a colliery line at Tangshan in China. The train's locomotive, a 2-6-2, is changing ends while the outgoing shift of miners climbs aboard.

ABOVE: A pair of QJ 2-10-2 locomotives climbing with a heavy freight at Lanxiang in Manchuria. The design is an improved version of a Soviet Railroad postwar 2-10-2, which was in production from 1956 into the late 1980s, with several thousand being built. This type is also sometimes used on passenger services.

RIGHT: One of the standard 0-8-0 locomotives used on Chinese narrow-gauge lines.

TOP RIGHT: A Pacific and a QJ at Changchun. The Pacific is of the RM type, built in the late 1950s and combining some Soviet features with an existing Japanese-designed Pacific. Passenger services were often the first to be dieselized in China, so in the early 1990s this class was fading out.

A 4-6-0 of the former Bombay Baroda and Central India Railway enters Vadodara (Baroda), as a WP Pacific prepares to leave.

LEFT: An industrial railroad in Spain. This shows tank locomotives attending the washing plant. In general, intermittent yard and assembly work is especially suitable for diesels, and many mainline railroads dieselized their yard operations first. On colliery lines this did not always happen, because fuel seemed so cheap, and in continental Europe a number still used steam traction in the 1980s.

BELOW: Even in western Germany a colliery at Aachen still used steam traction in the early 1990s.

RIGHT: This type of 2-8-2 was used by many Chinese industrial lines. The locomotive here is still in its works undercoat, having just been completed at the Tangshan locomotive works.

RIGHT: A Central Railway freight leaves Agra in India behind a 'MacArthur' 2-8-2. India received many of these locomotives during and after World War II. This one is of the CWD class, indicating that it was built by Canadian Locomotive or the Montreal Locomotive Works. Units built by US works were classified as AWD. The design became well-known as a US war-service type, and several other countries received it. Many are still in use in India and Pakistan.

LEFT: WG 2-8-2s passing at Patna, India. These were built from 1950 into the 1970s for heavy broad-gauge freight service, although they sometimes appeared on secondary passenger trains. Most were Indian-built, and the orders for imports were scattered among a variety of builders including Japanese, Italian, Austrian and Belgian. Fifty were built in the US by Baldwin. The overhead structure in this picture carries flexible pipes for watering passenger trains.

LEFT: A WP Pacific prepares to depart with a passenger train. By the 1990s these semi-streamlined Pacifics no longer hauled the major Indian passenger trains but found good use in secondary services. Their streamlining, which consisted mainly of a bullet nose, was said to be thereby rendered unnecessary. But this had always been true; the designers (Baldwin) had included it for aesthetic effect.

BELOW: Another Indian WP, this time in the colors of the Central Railway, which was mainly the former Great Indian Peninsular Railway. It was, and still is, usual for Indian locomotive men to keep their machines in immaculate order, with extra, personal, decorations sometimes added.

LEFT: 2ft 6in and 5ft 6in gauges cross near Baroda in western India. A WP Pacific is in charge of a Bombay-bound broad gauge train while a narrow-gauge mixed train, headed by an elderly 4-6-0, passes underneath. The extensive narrow-gauge system was owned by the Gaekwar of Baroda until 1949, when it became part of Indian Railways.

BELOW LEFT: American-style and British-style freight power in Bombay. On the left is a Canadian-built 'MacArthur' 2-8-2, while the 2-8-0 is a class G built by Armstrong Whitworth in the 1920s to a standard BESA (British Engineering Standards Association) design.

BELOW: Another BESA design for a 2-8-0, the H/4. Built in Scotland in 1914, this was larger than the G, opposite, having a bigger boiler, driving wheels of 56in rather than 54in diameter, and bigger cylinders. It is shown hauling the Ajni-Nagpur shuttle, a short-distance trip operated mainly for railway workers.

ABOVE: A highly-decorated Canadian-built 'MacArthur' 2-8-2 at rest and, as is often the case, becoming a source of boiling water for local inhabitants. This class of locomotive, supplied in the 1940s, has proved long-lasting and has a good chance of surviving until the turn of the century.

RIGHT: Standard locomotives of British India still at work at Peshawar in Pakistan. The 2-8-0 has just uncoupled from the weekly Khyber Pass train, a service into the rugged North-West Frontier on a line laid by British military engineers in the 1920s which goes up to the Afghanistan frontier.

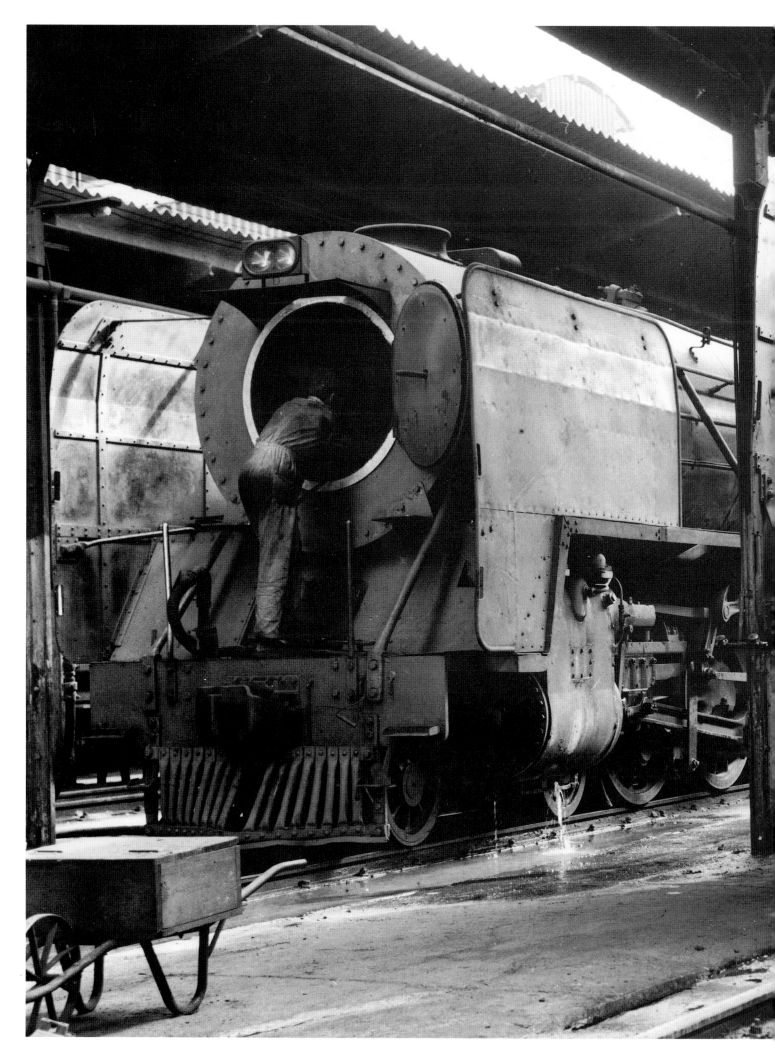

LEFT: Inside the locomotive depot at Bloemfontein. This was one of the last depots to operate South African steam traction in regular service; by 1993 active steam locomotives were to be operated either by a special subsidiary 'Transnet Museum' responsible for museum and tourist activity, or by industrial railways, which willingly acquired former mainline machines. The two units shown here are 4-8-4s, which had started life as condensing locomotives.

LEFT: One of the South African lines expected to retain steam traction for tourist and nostalgic reasons is the picturesque branch between George and Knysna. For such lightly-laid branches the South African railways bought several classes of light 4-8-2 and 2-8-4 locomotives. One of them is seen here on a freight near George.

BELOW: The South African Railways 'Red Devil' is a 4-8-4 rebuilt in 1980 with a gas-producer firebox, in which the fuel is kept at quite a low temperature, with most combustion taking place above it. Long trials indicated that this technology can improve efficiency, but it was not carried further in South Africa due to the existing commitment to dieselization.

LEFT: A pair of condensing 4-8-4s haul a freight train across the Great Karroo in South Africa. Few countries were so arid that they required condensing locomotives (locomotives that recycle their own water). The USSR was the biggest user. They used a smokebox fan to provide draft, since the steam no longer passed up the chimney.

BELOW LEFT: The same train, showing the special condenser tenders. Such locomotives did not puff — they whined like a jet engine, thanks to their smokebox fans. These 3ft 6in gauge 4-8-4s were eventually converted to orthodox locomotives.

BELOW: The 2ft 6in gauge lines from Port Elizabeth in South Africa witnessed the seasonal operation of two steam trains for tourists. One visited the harbor while the one shown in this picture, the 'Apple Express,' went into the fruit-growing hinterland.

ABOVE: A South African type GEA 4-8-2 + 2-8-4 Garratt at Oudtshoorn locomotive depot. These locomotives, built from 1946, hauled passenger as well as freight trains on the mountainous main line between Worcester and Oudtshoorn. Several different designs of Garratt were used in South Africa, as they were ideal for producing high power on small and well distributed axleloads. The type was still used in neighbouring Zimbabwe in the 1990s.

ABOVE RIGHT: Also off-duty at Oudtshoorn locomotive depot are a couple of 4-8-2s and a Garratt.

RIGHT: A 19D class 4-8-2 pulls out of Oudtshoorn with a branch train. This class, built in Britain from 1948, was a development of the original 19 class introduced in 1928. They had an axleload of less than 14 tons and this final batch had tenders that carried 6500 gallons of water and were as long as the locomotive itself.

ABOVE: "Clan Line," one of the larger 4-6-2 type introduced by the Southern Railway, rebuilt in non-streamlined form by British Railways, and now preserved. The picture shows it in excursion service in northern England, on the Settle and Carlisle line.

LEFT: The Dart Valley Railway in Devon is one of several British tourist railways that have their own large workshops.

RIGHT: "Duchess of Hamilton," built as a streamlined 4-6-2 in the 1930s, hauled the main Anglo-Scottish trains of the LMS, including the 'Coronation Scot.' Streamlining was removed in the 1940s and in the 1960s the locomotive was withdrawn and put on static display. Subsequently it was repaired and placed in excursion service. The picture shows it hauling an excursion on the Settle and Carlisle line.

246

LEFT: In the canefields of Queensland a 0-6-2 tank locomotive heads toward the refinery at Bundaberg. Except for special occasions, canefield steam traction is no longer used in Australia but can still be seen in Cuba, India and Indonesia.

BELOW LEFT: A K class 2-8-0 of Victorian Railways in excursion service. This type, designed and built in Australia, totaled 53 units and was regarded as an exceptionally trouble-free machine. The first appeared in 1922.

BELOW: As a vintage tram rumbles over the crossing, the timber roof of Ballarat's station frames a Victorian Railways K class 2-8-0, hauling one of the many steam tourist trains operated each year in Australia.

LEFT: On the North Yorkshire Moors Railway, which operates a regular summer service over a former LNER cross-country line, a 1949-built Mogul catches the evening sun.

248

BELOW LEFT: The 'Puffing Billy' tourist line near Melbourne. This is a resurrected 2ft 6in gauge line, which uses several of the 2-6-2 tank locomotives designed by Baldwin. The initial delivery from the US came in 1898, but subsequently this class was built at Melbourne.

BELOW: "Sir Lamiel," the only survivor of the Southern Railway's 'King Arthur' 4-6-0 class, once broke a speed record in its youth, but is now used in excursion service. It is shown serving a temporary spell on the Keighley and Worth Valley Railway. British tourist lines often exchange locomotives, and they are also allowed to use locomotives from the National Collection.

ABOVE: British railway enthusiast clubs sometimes join together to sponsor steam excursions. Ireland is often the scene, and this picture shows one of a class of five 4-4-0s built in 1913 for the Great Northern Railway of Ireland. Another of them, "Slieve Gullion," is preserved in working order. Painted blue, the 4-4-0 here is shown as it was owned by CIE, the company into which the GNR(I) was merged.

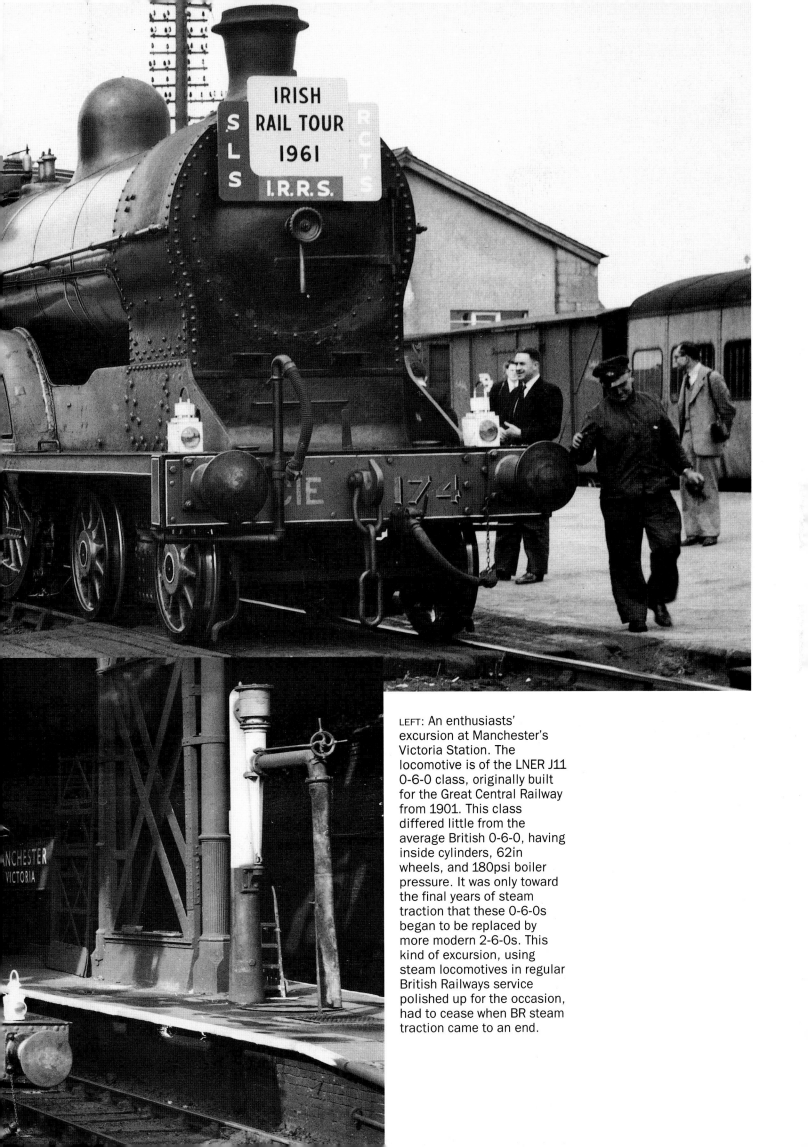

IRISH
RAIL TOUR
1961
S L S
R C T S
I.R.R.S.

CIE 174

NCHESTER
VICTORIA

LEFT: An enthusiasts' excursion at Manchester's Victoria Station. The locomotive is of the LNER J11 0-6-0 class, originally built for the Great Central Railway from 1901. This class differed little from the average British 0-6-0, having inside cylinders, 62in wheels, and 180psi boiler pressure. It was only toward the final years of steam traction that these 0-6-0s began to be replaced by more modern 2-6-0s. This kind of excursion, using steam locomotives in regular British Railways service polished up for the occasion, had to cease when BR steam traction came to an end.

ABOVE: Numerous tourist short lines operate in the US in summer, and in states where forestry was once important Shay type locomotives like this can often be seen.

ABOVE RIGHT: On the Strasburg Railroad in Pennsylvania an 0-6-0, once a yard locomotive, hauls a train of open-top passenger cars.

RIGHT: At the terminal of the Strasburg RR a 4-4-0, once the property of the Pennsylvania RR, changes ends, ready to take out the next service. The Strasburg RR is one of the oldest and most successful of the US tourist railroads, benefiting from proximity to the Pennsylvania state railroad museum as well as other, non-railroad attractions.

BELOW: One of several excursions run to celebrate the 150th anniversary of the GWR in 1985. A 'King,' the biggest GWR 4-6-0 type, leads the smallest, a 'Manor.'

BOTTOM: The New South Wales 'Vintage Train,' which takes part in ceremonies and celebrations throughout the state. The leading 4-4-0 is one of 68 imported from Britain in the 1870s and 1880s.

RIGHT: In 1970 a steam train ran for the first time the whole length of Australia from Sydney to Perth. Here it is near Bathurst, NSW, hauled by streamlined and non-streamlined C-38 Pacifics. Both these locomotives have since been preserved.

BELOW RIGHT: The first 4-6-2 design to work on Queensland Railways. Two of this class still haul tourist trains, and others are on static exhibition in the state. Like other Queensland-built designs, they resemble US locomotives but include British features.

ABOVE: The Russian E class 0-10-0, introduced before World War I, was still being built after World War II, and became the world's most numerous type. A few were still in service in the early 1990s. This example was photographed at the Osipovichi locomotive depot.

ABOVE RIGHT: Another view of one of the Soviet Railroad's E class 0-10-0s. Most of them were built in Russia, but some were imported from Sweden, Germany, and Hungary. In recent times, dozens have been put on plinths for permanent exhibition on, or near, railroad stations.

RIGHT: This is the postwar Soviet freight locomotive, a 2-10-0. As its running number indicates, several thousand of these were built, and some were still active in the early 1990s. Compared to other European railroads, locomotives were very tall in Russia, as is suggested by the big gap between boiler and chassis.

ABOVE LEFT: Another view of the postwar Soviet 2-10-0. The cylindrical Vanderbilt tender shows that it is one of the early units of the class.

LEFT: The SO type, is a prewar Soviet design of 2-10-0. By the early 1990s, surviving examples of this class were mainly confined to stationary service as heating boilers. The photograph shows how, in their prime, they were commonly used in pairs, because poor track and rising traffic meant that Soviet locomotives tended to be too small for the job.

ABOVE: Steam persisted in Hungary to the late 1980s. One of the most useful locomotives was this general duties Type 424 4-8-0. Introduced in 1924, several hundred were built, and some found their way to Russia, China and Yugoslavia. They were said to be superbly engineered and very competent machines. The Russian units were forcibly removed after World War II but were returned in the 1960s and restored to standard gauge. This locomotive has the Hungarian 'Ister' multiple-jet exhaust and double chimney.

MAIN PICTURE: One of the standard Soviet Railroad Su class 2-6-2s. A few of these have been kept for excursion service.

INSET: The postwar Polish passenger locomotive was also a 2-6-2, and a few of these were still in service in 1993.

ABOVE: In eastern Germany a Pacific (on the left) and a 2-8-2 stand at the buffer stops in Leipzig's main station. The Pacific is of a class rebuilt, with a bigger boiler, from the prewar 4-6-2.

LEFT: 180 of this Pt-47 2-8-2 design were produced at two Polish locomotive works after World War II, closely following a prewar design. They were used on principal passenger trains until electrification drove them to secondary services. A few were still active in the early 1990s.

ABOVE: A German prewar Pacific stands at Dresden with a Berlin train. This was one of the last European main routes to be served by steam traction. The locomotive is of a class designed by Richard Wagner and is a standard inter-war type. In keeping with the old Prussian tradition, maximum power per ton was not sought. This allowed priority for other virtues like ease of maintenance, durability, and low stress levels.

RIGHT: Examples of the German 'Kriegslok' 2-10-0, acquired by Soviet Railroad after World War II.

LEFT: The 3ft gauge Isle of Man Railway still operates in summer, using 80-year old Beyer Peacock 2-4-0 tank locomotives like this. Most of the extensive network has been closed, leaving a single route operating from Douglas to Port Erin.

RIGHT: Several narrow-gauge railroads are still providing services in eastern Germany. This postwar 2-10-2 tank locomotive is hauling a passenger train on a 2ft 6in gauge line south of Dresden.

BELOW: A former US Army 2-6-2 tank locomotive, a survivor of the US narrow-gauge Western Front railroads of World War I, now at work on the 2ft gauge Ffestiniog Railway in Wales.

266

LEFT: A network of narrow-gauge lines centered on Gmund in northern Austria until recently made extensive use of steam traction, but now steam is held only in reserve or for excursions. This is one of the 0-8-0s, with a typical passenger train.

BELOW LEFT: The Klaus-Garsten narrow gauge line in Austria was abandoned by the Austrian State Railways in the 1980s, but part has been resurrected as a tourist operation. This shows one of the trains on the now-closed part of the line.

BELOW: Another view of the Klaus-Garsten narrow gauge line in Austria. The 0-6-2 tank locomotive is of a standard design and may be found elsewhere in Austria.

NEXT PAGE: The Cumbres Pass and Toltec RR is one of the most scenic 3ft gauge railroads in the Rockies, and operates a summer tourist service. It uses 2-8-2 locomotives, and on some days doubleheading is necessary.

INDEX

ACKNOWLEDGMENTS

The author and publisher would like to thank Ron Callow, the designer; Stephen Small, the editor and picture researcher; Nicki Giles and Veronica Price, for production; Ron Watson for preparing the index; and the individuals and institutions listed below for supplying the pictures:

AGS/Alco Historic Photos, pages: 8(bottom), 12, 47(bottom), 164(bottom), 193(bottom)

AGS/California State Railroad Museum, pages: 38-9, 58, 184(bottom), 199(bottom)

AGS/Canadian Pacific, pages: 120(top)

AGS/C&O Railroad, pages: 70(top right), 121(bottom)

AGS/New York Central Historical Society, pages: 121(top)

AGS/PHMC Railroad Museum of Pennsylvania, pages: 26(top)

AGS/Santa Fe Railroad, pages: 6(top), 66, 117(bottom), 165(bottom), 189(bottom)

AGS/Smithsonian Institute, pages: 6(bottom), 55(bottom), 80(top), 97(top), 118(top), 172(top)

Association of American Railroads, pages: 128

H.L. Broadbelt, pages: 187(top), 189(top & middle)

Brompton Books, pages: 23(top), 26(bottom), 27, 29(bottom), 36(bottom), 43, 47(top), 51(top), 52(bottom), 56(bottom), 67(bottom & middle), 68(bottom), 81(both), 100(top), 116(top left), 126-7, 128-9, 115(top), 163(bottom), 164(top), 168(bottom), 178(top), 180(top), 185(bottom), 186(bottom), 187(bottom), 189(top), 214(top), 238-9(both)

Canadian National Railroad, pages: 126-7

Chicago Historical Society, pages: 128-9

M.Deane, pages: 62(bottom), 98(bottom), 107, 146-7

T. Heywood, pages: 171(top), 256, 260-1

Hulton Deutsch Collection, pages: 18(bottom), 22, 23(bottom), 24(bottom), 25(top), 35(top), 62(top), 63(top), 67(top), 104(top), 114(both), 115(all three), 133(bottom), 137(bottom), 149(top), 157(top), 188(bottom)

Jury Iljin, pages: 258(top), 263(bottom)

K.P. Lawrence, pages: 248(bottom)

Lifefile, pages: 130(bottom/Bill Webster), 244(bottom)

Milwaukee Railroad, pages: 165(top)

National Railway Museum, pages: 9(bottom), 13(top), 16, 17(bottom), 18, 20(top), 31(bottom), 34-5, 44-5, 49(top), 68(top), 75(bottom), 99(top), 111(bottom)

South African Transport Services, pages: 184(middle)

TRH, pages: 38(top), 65, 69(top left), 73(both), 85(all three), 88(bottom), 89, 97(bottom), 101(bottom), 108(top), 124(bottom), 130(top), 133(top), 167(bottom), 176(bottom), 188(middle), 194(bottom), 197(bottom), 230-1(both), 234-5, 250-1(both)

V/line, Australia, pages: 9(top), 19, 69(bottom), 116(bottom), 137(top)

John Westwood, pages: 8(top & middle), 13(top), 14(both), 15, 17(top), 20(bottom), 25(bottom), 28(bottom), 28-9, 30, 31(top), 32(both), 33, 34(top), 39(top), 40, 41(both), 42(both), 44(top), 45(top), 46, 48(bottom), 50, 51(bottom), 52(top), 53, 54(bottom), 54-5, 56-7, 57(bottom), 59, 60-1(all three), 63(bottom), 64(both), 68(middle), 69(top right), 70(top left), 71(both), 72(both), 76(top), 82-3, 84(both), 86, 87(top), 88(top), 90(both), 91, 92(all three), 93(both), 94(both), 95, 96, 97(middle), 98(top), 99(bottom), 100(middle & bottom), 101(top), 103(bottom), 104(bottom), 105, 106(all three), 108(bottom), 109(all three), 110(both), 112(both), 113(both), 116(top right), 117(top), 118(top), 120(bottom), 123(bottom), 124(top), 125(both), 126(bottom), 132, 134(top), 136, 140-1(both), 142, 143(both), 144(both), 145, 148(both), 149(bottom), 151(both), 152(bottom), 153(both), 154, 155(bottom), 156(both), 157(bottom), 159(bottom), 160(top), 161(both), 162(bottom), 162-3, 167(top), 168(top), 169(both), 170-1, 172(bottom), 173, 176(top), 177(all three), 178(middle & bottom), 179(both), 180(middle), 180-1, 181(top), 182(both), 185(top), 188(top), 190(both), 192(top & middle), 193, 194(top), 195(top), 196(both), 197(top), 198(top), 200(both), 201(all three), 202(both), 204, 206(top), 207, 208, 209, 212, 213(both), 215(both), 216-7, 218-9(both), 220, 221(both), 222-3(all three), 224-5, 226(both), 227, 229(both), 232(both), 233, 235(bottom), 236-7, 240(both), 242-3(all three), 246-7(all three), 253(both), 254(both), 255(both), 257(both), 258(bottom), 259(top), 260(top), 262(both), 263(top), 264(both), 265, 266(both), 267

Jim Winkley, pages: 1, 2(both), 3, 4, 5(both), 7(top), 10(both), 11(both), 21, 24(top), 36-7, 48(top), 74(all three), 75(top), 76(bottom), 77(both), 78-9, 102-3, 111(top), 119, 122-3, 134-5, 138-9, 150, 158-9, 161(bottom), 166, 174, 175, 183, 186(top), 191, 195(bottom), 203(all four), 205, 206(bottom), 210-11, 214(bottom), 226(top), 244-5, 245(bottom), 248(top), 249, 252(top), 268-9